Treasures

Practice
Book

Macmillan/McGraw-Hill

B

The *McGraw·Hill* Companies

Macmillan/McGraw-Hill

Published by Macmillan/McGraw-Hill, of McGraw-Hill Education, a division of The McGraw-Hill Companies, Inc., Two Penn Plaza, New York, New York 10121.

Printed in the United States of America

2 3 4 5 6 7 8 9 RHR 14 13 12 11 10

Contents

Unit 1 • Taking a Stand

Contents

Unit 2 • Investigations

Contents

Unit 3 • Using Your Wits

Contents

Unit 4 • Team Up to Survive

Contents

Unit 5 • The American West

© Macmillan/McGraw-Hill

Contents

Unit 6 • Changes

Name _____

The letters *a*, *e*, *i*, *o*, and *u* sometimes stand for the short vowel sounds /a/ in *damp*, /e/ in *ten*, /i/ in *sit*, /o/ in *hop*, and /u/ in *fun*. Some words with short vowel sounds do not follow this pattern. For example, *ea*, as in *head*, can have the /e/ sound, and *ou* followed by *gh*, as in *rough*, can have the /u/ sound.

Place each word in the column that describes the short vowel sound found in the word.

batch	rough	stump	jut	tenth
love	myth	nick	sense	cot
bread	notch	scan	tough	damp
lot	stamp	sick	fence	rhythm

short *a*	short *e*	short *i*	short *o*	short *u*
_____	_____	_____	_____	_____
_____	_____	_____	_____	_____
_____	_____	_____	_____	_____
_____	_____	_____	_____	_____
_____	_____	_____	_____	_____
_____	_____	_____	_____	_____
_____	_____	_____	_____	_____
_____	_____	_____	_____	_____

© Macmillan/McGraw-Hill

Name _____

A. Match the vocabulary word with its definition. Then write the correct word on the line.

blurted	permission	scald	autograph
fare	spectacular	clenched	approached

1. sensational, fantastic _____

2. burn _____

3. spoke suddenly _____

4. came near _____

5. closed together tightly _____

6. consent _____

7. a person's signed name _____

8. price charged for public transportation _____

B. Write a paragraph using at least three vocabulary words. Underline each vocabulary word you use.

_____

_____

_____

_____

_____

_____

_____

_____

_____

_____

When you summarize a story, describe the **characters** (people or animals in the story), **setting** (where and when the story happens), and select important plot events such as the conflicts the characters face and the relationships they have with each other and situations in the story. Organize these descriptions in your own words. Identifying each character's role and function can help you better understand a story's plot.

Read this story, and then summarize it. Include information about the characters, setting, and how they relate to the plot.

'Tricia Ann listened carefully to her grandmother, Mama Frances. Everyone listened carefully to Mama Frances because the old woman was wise, strong, and had a no-nonsense attitude. She also had a huge heart.

" 'Tricia Ann," Mama Frances said, "it's your first trip alone downtown. Don't let anyone give you what-for, you hear? You keep going to Someplace Special with your head held high." Mama Frances was determined to boost her granddaughter's pride and self-confidence.

'Tricia Ann walked through the city. She saw sign after sign proclaiming Whites Only and Colored Section. White people glared at her as she passed them on the sidewalk. She wanted to run home crying. But 'Tricia Ann held her head high and walked bravely through the city streets.

Finally, she was there! 'Tricia Ann climbed the steps to the public library, her very own special place, where everyone was welcome. She knew that Mama Frances was right: March proudly, and you will get to where you want to go.

Summary: _____

_____

_____

_____

_____

Name _____

As you read *Goin' Someplace Special*, fill in the Character and
Setting Chart. Include information about the characters' roles in the story.

Character	Setting

How does the information you wrote in the Character and Setting Chart
help you analyze the story structure of *Goin' Someplace Special*?

© Macmillan/McGraw-Hill

As I read, I will pay attention to my expression and accuracy.

8	Josie and Franklin had heard Gramma's stories many times, but they never got tired of them. There was something
19	so comforting about Gramma's voice. Josie felt as if she were
30	being wrapped in a warm, fuzzy blanket when she listened to
41	Gramma's stories. And even though Franklin was 14 going
49	on 15, he still liked to hear Gramma's stories about her life in
61	the South.
63	Now Franklin got up from the step where he had been
74	sitting. "Gramma, I have to go do my math homework. I'll
85	see you at dinner."
89	Josie stayed where she was. Like Gramma, Josie loved
98	nature, but living in the city didn't provide much. She looked
109	around the neighborhood. Outside their second-floor
115	apartment, Gramma had planted window boxes, bright with
123	red and white geraniums. Other than that, a few spindly trees
134	that grew between the sidewalk and the curb were the only
145	green, growing things that Josie could see.
152	Other neighbors were sitting on their front stoops, too,
161	hoping for a cool evening breeze. 167

Comprehension Check

1. Why does Josie enjoy listening to Gramma's stories? **Plot Development**

2. What do Josie and her grandmother have in common? **Main Idea and Details**

	Words Read	–	Number of Errors	=	Words Correct Score
First Read		–		=	
Second Read		–		=	

© Macmillan/McGraw-Hill

Name _____

When you read a story, you think about the characters and the setting. The setting can be the present time, or it can be another historical period. The setting and the historic events that surround it often affect the story's **theme**. A theme is the message about life that the author wants readers to understand.

Read this story. Then answer the questions.

Raul stepped out into the garden one morning with his father. "Tell me again why we have a garden, Dad," he said.

"Well, there are many reasons. You know that America is in a big war, and President Roosevelt thinks that Victory Gardens are important. If we grow our own food, the food we no longer need to buy can help feed soldiers. Many of the farmers are in the army now, too," Raul's father said as he picked up a big squash. "This will taste good tonight!"

"Wow, did you see how big our pumpkin is? I can't wait to have pumpkin pie," Raul said.

"You seem to enjoy watching things grow. Let's check for tomatoes and corn before we go in," Dad added.

"Yes, it's fun to watch plants grow, but the best part is knowing that our garden helps end the war," Raul said.

1. What is the theme of this passage?

   _____

   _____

2. How does the historic event affect the theme?

   _____

   _____

Name _____

A **time line** is a diagram that organizes information. Time lines help you keep track of events in the order in which they took place.

Look at the time line. Then answer the questions.

Important Civil Rights Dates

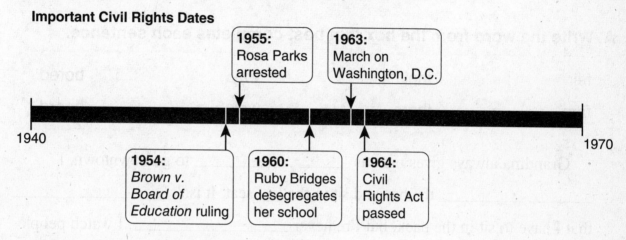

1955: Rosa Parks arrested

1963: March on Washington, D.C.

1940   1970

1954: *Brown v. Board of Education* ruling

1960: Ruby Bridges desegregates her school

1964: Civil Rights Act passed

1. What is this time line about? _____

_____

2. What happened in 1955? _____

3. What happened first: the Civil Rights Act or the *Brown* v. *Board of Education* ruling? _____

4. In which city did civil rights protesters march in 1963? _____

5. Would Rosa Parks have been arrested for refusing to give up her seat after 1964? Explain your answer. _____

_____

6. Where would this event appear on the time line? In 1946, the United States Supreme Court bans segregation on buses that travel across state lines.

_____

_____

> **Homophones** are words that sound the same but have different spellings and different meanings. Sometimes you need to read the words around a homophone to know which spelling and meaning makes the most sense.

A. Write the word from the box that best completes each sentence.

fair	their	way	bored
fare	there	weigh	board

Grandma always gives me bus _____ to go downtown. I

_____ the bus and sit in the last seat. It isn't _____

that I have to sit in the back, but I'm never _____. I watch people

carry _____ packages. Those bundles must _____

so much! I ride the bus all the _____ to the library. I'm so happy

when I'm _____.

B. Circle the two homophones in each sentence. Then answer the question.

1. The wind blew my blue hat away.

   Which word refers to a color? _____

2. I had to write the right word for each item on the test.

   Which word means "correct"? _____

3. Marta took one more turn and won the spelling bee.

   Which word means that someone has gained victory? _____

4. It is great to live in our state's capital because we can visit the capitol any time.

   Which word refers to a building? _____

A. Reading Strategy: Set a Purpose for Reading

As you read, think about your purpose for reading. You might set your own purpose for reading, or your teacher might set a purpose for you. Choose a text that you will read this week, and complete the activity.

Before Reading Circle the phrase that best completes the statement.

My purpose is to . . .

be entertained.   think about life or how people act.

learn about something.   find out how to do something.

form an opinion about something.   make a decision about something.

After Reading Complete the statement.

Because I read to _____,

I better understood _____

_____

_____.

B. Independent Reading Log

Choose something you would like to read. After reading, complete the reading log. Be sure to paraphrase, or tell the main idea or meaning of the text. Keep the details or events in the correct order. You may use the log to talk to others about what you read.

Genre _____

Title _____

Author _____

This Text Is About _____

_____

_____

_____

Words that have the VCe pattern usually have a **long vowel** sound, as in *fame*, *mine*, and *bone*. The vowel digraphs *ai* and *ay* usually stand for the long *a* sound, as in *pail* and *play*. The digraphs *ee* and *ea* stand for the long *e* sound, as in *see* and *heap*. The digraphs *oa* and *ow* can stand for the long *o* sound, as in *boat* and *flow*. The vowel *i* can stand for the long *i* sound in words such as *wind* and *wild*. The letters *igh* in *high* can also stand for the long *i* sound.

A. Write the words from the box that have the same long vowel sound as the first word in each row. Underline the letters that make the long vowel sound.

coach	bike	wheat	pain	may	deep
steam	flight	slate	towing	mind	float

1. rake _____ _____

2. feet _____ _____

3. kite _____ _____

4. flow _____ _____ _____

B. Write a sentence using as many long vowel sound words as possible.

_____

_____

_____

_____

Name _____

A. Use the correct word from the list to complete each sentence.

injury   mournful   sympathy   delivering
couple   shrieks   decency

1. The mother felt _____ toward the hurt hawk.

2. Did you hear the _____ of all those birds?

3. I saw them _____ the hawk to the veterinarian.

4. The hawk had suffered an _____ but was going to survive.

5. The mother and child had the _____ to stop the car and take care of the hawk.

6. People can become very _____ when they see injured animals.

7. I hope the bird will get well in a _____ of days.

B. Use the vocabulary words to answer the questions.

8. **shrieks** What do shrieks sound like?

_____

_____

9. **mournful** What does it mean to be mournful?

_____

_____

10. **decency** What are some ways people show decency?

_____

_____

© Macmillan/McGraw-Hill

Name _____

Making inferences can help you better understand the **plot development** of a story. To make inferences, use story clues and your own related knowledge that connects to the story. Then you make a logical decision about story events not directly stated in the text, but that contribute to the development of the plot.

Read the selection. Then make inferences to answer the questions.

Maria walked into the kitchen with a frown on her face. Her mother was standing over the counter, chopping red peppers. Maria sat down on a small stool.

Maria's mother looked up from her cutting board. "Maria, you need to cheer up. Rowdy wasn't your dog. It's not fair for you to keep him."

"I know," Maria began. "I'll be all right. I'll just miss when Rowdy jumps on my belly when I'm lying on the floor. I'll miss when he curls up in that shoe box. I'll just miss him."

Maria's mother stopped chopping and walked over beside her daughter. "Sweetie, don't you worry. Your birthday is right around the corner, and I know just what to get you."

Maria's face lit up. "Oh, Mom!" she exclaimed, hugging her mother.

1. How is Maria feeling in the beginning of the story? How do you know?

_____

2. How is Maria feeling at the end of the story? How do you know?

_____

3. How big is Rowdy? How do you know?

_____

4. What do you think will happen on Maria's birthday?

_____

© Macmillan/McGraw-Hill

Name _____

As you read *Shiloh*, fill in the Inferences Chart.

Text Clues	What You Know	Inferences

How does the information you wrote in this Inferences Chart help you analyze the story structure of *Shiloh*?

© Macmillan/McGraw-Hill

As I read, I will pay attention to my intonation.

	Just past the admissions window, not far from a display of
11	llamas, Mrs. Battaglia assembled her students. She blew her
20	nose, cleared her throat, and said, "There are ten endangered
30	animals here at the zoo. *Achoo!*"
36	"Bless you," someone muttered.
40	"Thank you. In groups of three, you are to visit them and
52	answer all of the questions on your worksheet."
60	Alice noticed that Mrs. Battaglia's eyes were red and
69	tearing. She glanced at Wendy, who giggled. For all her talk
80	about their fascinating blood cells, Mrs. Battaglia was clearly
89	too allergic to go anywhere near actual animals.
97	"At the end of today, your group will choose one—*achoo!*—
108	animal. It will be your assignment to find a way to raise
120	money for that animal at the school fundraiser in two weeks."
131	Wendy grabbed Alice's hand. "Let's go together," she
139	said. 140

Comprehension Check

1. What does *allergic* mean in this passage? **Context Clues**

2. How do you think Mrs. Battaglia feels about the field trip to the zoo?
   Plot Development

	Words Read	–	Number of Errors	=	Words Correct Score
First Read		–		=	
Second Read		–		=	

Name _____

Sometimes a writer shows meaning by using **literary language and devices** such as **similes** and **metaphors**. A simile uses the words *like* or *as* to compare two unlike things. A metaphor also compares two unlike things but does not use *like* or *as*. Information from literary devices helps you make inferences.

Read the passage below. Then complete the chart.

Like a kangaroo, I jumped out of bed on Saturday morning. I threw on an old shirt and pants and ran to breakfast. Soon, I was riding my bike to the animal shelter.

The shelter was a circus of sights and sounds. Rick, the head volunteer, smiled like the sun at me. I could hear barking and meows from the back room. Puppies tumbled like clowns when I opened their cages. Tongues of sandpaper lapped at my hands. The morning flew by as I filled bowls and changed papers.

Too soon, it was time to leave. "Can you come back next week?" Rick asked. "I would love to!" I said.

Words From Story	Literary Device	Inferences

What inference can you make about the narrator's morning from the information you wrote in the chart? _____

_____

© Macmillan/McGraw-Hill

A **photograph** can help you see what a story or article is explaining or describing. The photograph's **caption** provides more information about what you see in the photograph.

Look at the photograph, read the caption, and then put a check next to the statements that would be included in an article written about this picture.

People come to choose and adopt animals at the animal shelter.

1. _____ Ten dogs, five cats, seven kittens, and twelve puppies were adopted in all.

2. _____ The Lions Club will be holding their annual fair on July 30.

3. _____ There was a clown giving out balloons and a cowboy offering free pony rides.

4. _____ There was an Adoption Fair at the Third Street animal shelter today.

5. _____ Eleven-year-old Richard Vitarelli went home with a beagle pup.

6. _____ People were encouraged to take prospective pets out of their crates and get acquainted with the animals.

Name _____

An **idiom** is a phrase that cannot be understood from the
meaning of the separate words in it. An **adage** is an old saying
that is a rule for something in life. You can often find the meanings
of idioms and adages in the dictionary. Being able to identify and
explain these and other sayings will improve your comprehension.

**A. Match each idiom, adage, or other saying to what it means. Then write
the correct letter on the line provided.**

1. _____ at the eleventh hour

2. _____ you live, you learn

3. _____ jump to a conclusion

4. _____ better late than never

a. decide something quickly without
thinking about it

b. it is better to arrive late than not at all

c. mistakes can teach useful lessons

d. at the last minute

**B. Circle the idiom, adage, or other saying in each sentence. Write the
meaning of the saying on the next line.**

5. I always remind myself that an apple a day keeps the doctor away when I
pick out my lunch in the cafeteria.

_____

6. Don't beat around the bush, just answer the question.

_____

7. Knowing that too many cooks spoil the broth, I only asked one friend to help
me build the boat.

_____

_____

8. You can ask until you're blue in the face, but I'm not trading you that
baseball card.

_____

_____

Name _____

A. Reading Strategy: Set a Purpose for Reading

As you read, think about your purpose for reading. You might set your own purpose for reading, or your teacher might set a purpose for you. Choose a text that you will read this week, and complete the chart.

Before Reading: My purpose for reading is...	After Reading: My purpose for reading helped me...

B. Independent Reading Log

Choose something you would like to read. After reading, complete the reading log. Be sure to paraphrase, or to tell the main idea or meaning of the text. Keep the details or events in the correct order. You may use the log to talk to others about what you read.

Genre _____

Title _____

Author _____

This Text Is About _____

_____

_____

_____

_____

Name _____

- The vowel **u** in **tuna**, the vowels **oo** in **soon**, and the letters **ew** in **grew** can stand for the **/ü/** sound. The VCe pattern in **plume** can also stand for the **/ü/** sound.
- The vowel **u** in **music**, the vowels **ue** in **cue**, the letters **ew** in **few**, and the VCe pattern in **cute** can also stand for the **/ū/** sound.
- The vowels **oo** can also stand for the **/ù/** sound in **book**.

Read each sentence. Circle the word that has the same vowel sound that you hear in *loon*, *mule*, or *book*. Then write the word in the column for that vowel sound.

1. It is important to prune a tree's branches.

2. Don't fasten those hooks to the tree branches!

3. The wildfire has a deep yellow hue.

4. My handbook about trees has great pictures.

5. We plant a few trees in the park each year.

6. Some flutes are made from trees.

7. This tree will provide wood for the people.

8. There are many ways to use that timber.

9. The horse carried the food up the hill.

l<u>oo</u>n /ü/	**m<u>u</u>l<u>e</u>** /ū/	**b<u>oo</u>k** /ù/

© Macmillan/McGraw-Hill

Name _____

Write a clue for each word in the crossword puzzle below.
Make each clue a sentence with a blank where the word in the
puzzle could go.

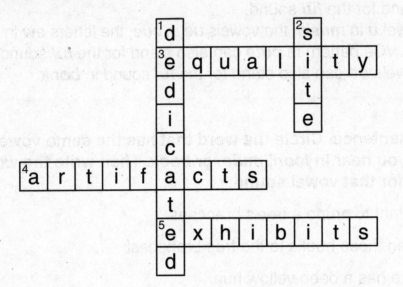

Across

3. _____
   _____

4. _____
   _____

5. _____
   _____

Down

1. _____
   _____

2. _____
   _____

Name _____

> The **main idea** is what all of the details in a paragraph or passage have in common. It is what the text is mostly about. When you summarize a passage, you should include the main idea and supporting details in your own words.

A. Read the paragraphs below. Then write the details on the lines provided and use them to determine the main idea.

Maya Lin is an architect who has designed several important monuments and memorials in the United States. She has a special talent for creating spaces that touch people's emotions. Lin's works honor people who were part of history.

Lin's Vietnam Veterans Memorial Wall has become the most visited monument in Washington, D.C. The memorial is a large black granite wall with names carved into the stone. Not everyone liked the memorial at first. However, it eventually helped many veterans and their families by honoring those who served.

Details: _____

_____

_____

Main idea: _____

_____

B. Now summarize the entire passage in your own words. Use the main idea and details of the paragraphs in your summary.

Summary: _____

_____

_____

_____

_____

Name _____

As you read "Maya Lin, Architect of Memory," fill in the Main Idea and Details Chart.

Detail
Detail
Detail
Main Idea

How does the information you wrote in this Main Idea and Details Chart help you summarize "Maya Lin, Architect of Memory"?

As I read, I will pay attention to phrasing.

	Why did so many people leave their homes? Why did they
11	leave behind everything they knew? Why did they risk their
21	lives and their families' lives to come to the United States?
32	Many were escaping hunger, poverty, or religious and
40	political persecution. The United States was their land of
49	hope. Many thought the streets were paved with gold. That's
59	why Ellis Island is called the "Golden Doors." Today's Ellis
69	Island is a museum honoring this important part of our
79	history.
80	To most immigrants, the United States was the land of
90	opportunity. It was a place where **equality** for all was
100	possible. To get there, people saved everything they earned to
110	buy a ticket on a ship. Some came alone and bid their
122	families farewell forever. Others saved enough to bring their
131	families. For most immigrants, the preparation and the
139	journey were not easy. 143

Comprehension Check

1. What are some reasons immigrants came to America? **Main Idea and Details**

2. What is the main idea of this passage? **Main Idea and Details**

	Words Read	–	Number of Errors	=	Words Correct Score
First Read		–		=	
Second Read		–		=	

Name _____

A **time line** is a diagram that shows several events in the order in which they happened. A time line helps readers understand factual information in an easy, visual way. Readers can also use a time line to get an overview of events and to locate specific information.

Use the time line below to answer the questions.

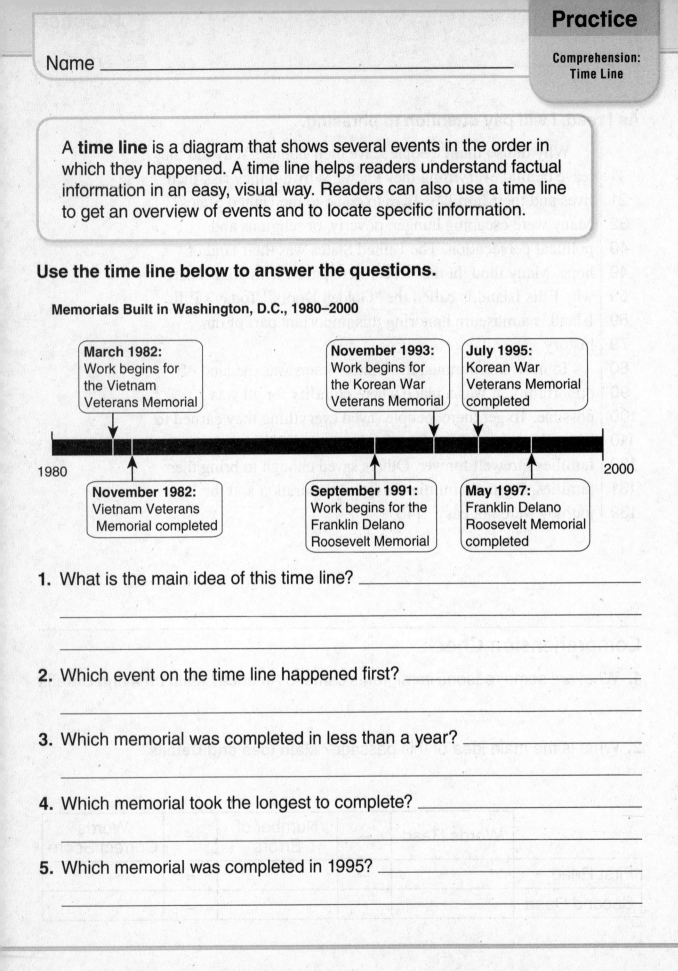

Memorials Built in Washington, D.C., 1980–2000

March 1982:
Work begins for the Vietnam Veterans Memorial

November 1993:
Work begins for the Korean War Veterans Memorial

July 1995:
Korean War Veterans Memorial completed

1980   2000

November 1982:
Vietnam Veterans Memorial completed

September 1991:
Work begins for the Franklin Delano Roosevelt Memorial

May 1997:
Franklin Delano Roosevelt Memorial completed

1. What is the main idea of this time line? _____

_____

_____

2. Which event on the time line happened first? _____

_____

3. Which memorial was completed in less than a year? _____

_____

4. Which memorial took the longest to complete? _____

_____

5. Which memorial was completed in 1995? _____

_____

Maya Lin, Architect of Memory
Grade 5/Unit 1

Name _____

> The **Internet** offers many online resources for research. Search
> engines are tools that enable you to search the Internet for
> information about a subject. You can use key words in a search
> engine to find information.

Use the Internet entries below to answer the questions.

1. Castle Clinton National Monument (National Park Service)
   Write to 26 Wall Street, New York, NY 10005.
   www.nps.gov/cacl/

2. The Immigration Experience
   Castle Garden, also known as Castle Clinton, was New York's first official immigration
   center. www.nyc.gov/html/nyc100/html/imm_stories/museum/

3. Clinton Castle—New York State Military Museum and Veterans Research Center
   Castle Clinton was one of more than a dozen forts built to defend New York Harbor.
   www.dmna.state.ny.us/forts/fortsA_D/clintonCastle.htm

1. What would be key words to use in a search engine to find information

   about this place? _____

   _____

2. Which Web site could you visit to learn about the military history of Castle

   Clinton? _____

   _____

3. Which Web site could you visit to learn about immigrants who went through

   Castle Clinton? _____

   _____

4. Which Web site could you visit to learn when Castle Clinton became a

   national monument? _____

   _____

© Macmillan/McGraw-Hill

You can change the form of a word by adding an **inflected ending** such as **-ed** or **-ing**. The inflected ending **-ed** is added to a verb to show that something happened in the past. The inflected ending **-ing** is added to a verb to show that something is happening in the present.

Remember these spelling rules:

1. If the base word ends with a consonant, double the final consonant before adding **-ed** or **-ing**.
2. If the base word ends in **y**, change the **y** to **i** before adding **-ed**.
3. If the base word ends in silent **e**, drop the **e** before adding **-ed** or **-ing**.

Add inflected endings to the words in parentheses, and write the new words on the lines.

Our family is (take) _____ a vacation in Washington, D.C.

As I research the city, I am (list) _____ how many sites

there are to visit. I am (plan) _____ to see many monuments

and memorials. (See) _____ the Lincoln Memorial is

an exciting thought. I am going (jog) _____ past the

Washington Monument. There are new places to visit, such as the National

Museum of the American Indian. I (ask) _____ my best

friend for her ideas about fascinating places to go. She said that I should

see the Vietnam Veterans Memorial wall. Apparently, many people (cry)

_____ when they visited the Vietnam Veterans Memorial

wall. I have (log) _____ all my research notes in a journal that

I will take on our trip.

Name _____

A. Reading Strategy: Set a Purpose for Reading

As you read, think about your purpose for reading. You might set your own purpose for reading, or your teacher might set a purpose for you. Choose a text that you will read this week, and answer the questions.

What is the title? _____

What is the topic? _____

What do you already know or think about this topic? _____

_____

_____

What do you want to know about this topic? _____

_____

_____

What is your purpose for reading this text? _____

_____

B. Independent Reading Log

Choose something you would like to read. After reading, complete the reading log. Be sure to paraphrase, or tell the main idea or meaning of the text. Keep the details or events in the correct order. You may use the log to talk to others about what you read.

Genre _____

Title _____

Author _____

This Text Is About _____

_____

_____

_____

- The letters *ar* usually stand for the /är/ sound in *car* and *carve*.
- The letters *ear* and *are* can stand for the /âr/ sound in *bear* and *care*.
- The letters *or*, *ore*, *oar*, and *our* can stand for the /ôr/ sound in *for*, *core*, *roar*, and *your*.

A. Underline the words in the paragraph that have the /är/ sound as in *car*, the /âr/ sound as in *bear*, or the /ôr/ sound as in *for*.

The astronauts climbed aboard their spaceship. They wore spacesuits made from special fabric. Their goal was to travel far into space and explore a nearby star. During the flight, they had many chores to do. They also had to take care not to tear holes in their suits.

B. Sort the underlined words in the paragraph according to the vowel + *r* sound.

/är/ sound in *car*	/âr/ sound in *bear*	/ôr/ sound in *for*
_____	_____	_____
_____	_____	_____
_____	_____	_____
_____	_____	_____

Name _____

A. From the box, choose a vocabulary word with a meaning similar to the underlined word or words in each sentence. Write the vocabulary word on the line provided.

forbidden	reluctant	mischievous	hesitation
purchased	gossiped	elegant	irresistible

1. Without <u>a pause</u>, I agreed to travel with my mother to Puerto Rico.
   _____

2. I was <u>unwilling</u> to give up another day of the trip. _____

3. I <u>talked casually</u> with friends about my aunts and uncles in Puerto Rico.
   _____

4. We <u>bought</u> a magazine from the newsstand.
   _____

5. The woman's <u>tasteful, stylish</u> outfit caught our attention.
   _____

6. The urge to talk to her was <u>impossible to ignore</u>. _____

7. I tried to keep quiet because talking to strangers was <u>not allowed</u>.
   _____

8. The <u>naughty</u> children made faces at the people walking past.
   _____

B. Write new sentences for two of the vocabulary words used above. Then underline the vocabulary word.

9. _____
   _____

10. _____
    _____

Name _____

Characters will often face a **problem** throughout a story. Their efforts to **solve** this problem show you the characters' traits. By recognizing the **problem and solution**, you will learn more about the characters.

Read the story below. Then answer the questions.

Kaitlin put her food tray on the table, looked at her watch, and said, "Ten minutes to eat again!" Janell mumbled between bites of her sandwich, "What else is new?"

Tearing through the sandwich wrapper, Kaitlin felt angry. It wasn't fair that the line was always so long. There had to be something she could do to change things. Kaitlin looked around and counted three workers in the cafeteria. Millie was at the cash register and Alice and Mo were behind the counter dishing out the casserole even though most kids ordered cold sandwiches on Fridays. Suddenly Kaitlin said, "I'm going to write a letter to Mrs. Bromley."

Janell gasped, "The principal? Kaitlin, are you serious?"

"I certainly am," Kaitlin answered. "I don't know how much money the school has, but I hope there's enough for another cash register."

1. Who is the main character in the story?

_____

2. What problem does the main character have?

_____

_____

3. What solution does the main character come up with?

_____

_____

© Macmillan/McGraw-Hill

Name _____

As you read *The Night of San Juan*, fill in the Story Map.

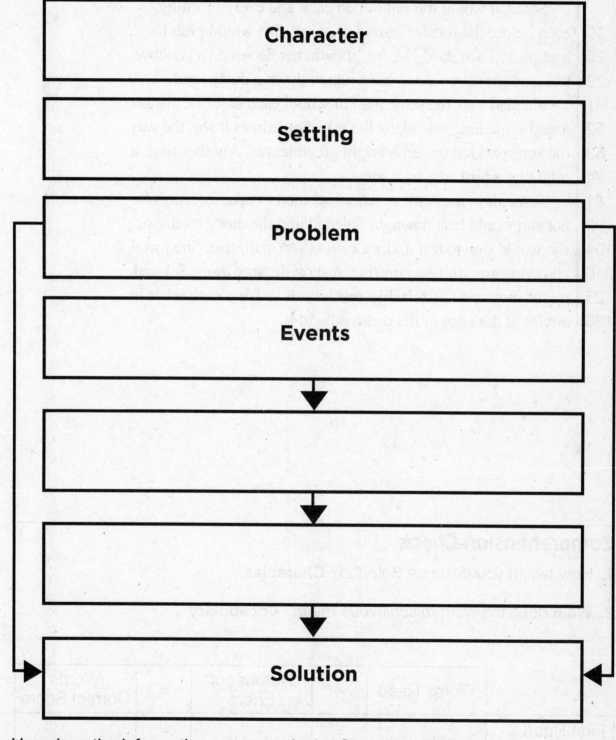

Character

Setting

Problem

Events

Solution

How does the information you wrote in the Story Map help you
summarize *The Night of San Juan*?

As I read, I will pay attention to expression and phrasing.

	Soledad would roll out of bed each and every morning,
10	even before the rooster started crowing. She would grab her
20	backpack. Then she'd give her grandfather Sebastián a goodbye
29	kiss and set off on a one-hour march down a dusty road.
41	Soledad took the same road to school each day. She always
52	found something new along the way. Sometimes it was the way
63	the sun sparkled on some bright green leaves. Another time it
74	might be a bird singing a song.
81	Some days the walk to school seemed to take forever. The
92	hot sun would beat down on Soledad and the dusty road. So,
104	she would stop to rest under a *ceiba* (SAY-bah) tree. She loved
116	observing everything around her. A short distance away, Soledad
125	might spot a pair of **mischievous** lizards chasing each other in
136	circles at the edge of the dirt road. 144

Comprehension Check

1. How would you describe Soledad? **Character**

2. What does the word *mischievous* mean? **Vocabulary**

	Words Read	–	Number of Errors	=	Words Correct Score
First Read		–		=	
Second Read		–		=	

Graphs summarize information that is in numbers. Graphs are often paired with written information that explains the numbers.

Look at the graph, and read the text. Then answer the questions.

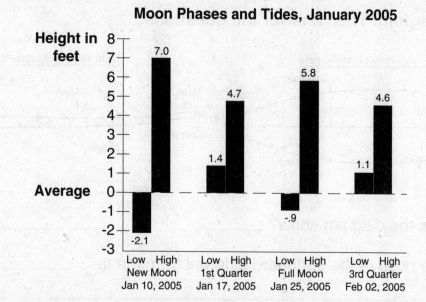

Moon Phases and Tides, January 2005

This bar graph shows the effect of the moon on tides. The bars on the graph show the height of the tides on four different days. The dotted horizontal line shows the average height of water at low tide. Sometimes the water may be lower than average. The longest bar below average shows the lowest tide recorded on these four days. The longest bar above average shows the highest tide. Some beach activities are influenced by the tides. Fishing and surfing are better at high tide. Finding clams is easier during low tide.

1. Which day would be the best day to go fishing? Why? _____

   _____

2. Using information from the text, what effect would a low tide have on your search for new sea shells? _____

   _____

Name _____

A **diagram** is a graphic aid that shows information. The important
parts of the diagram are labeled. A diagram can help readers
make comparisons.

Read the diagram. Then answer the questions.

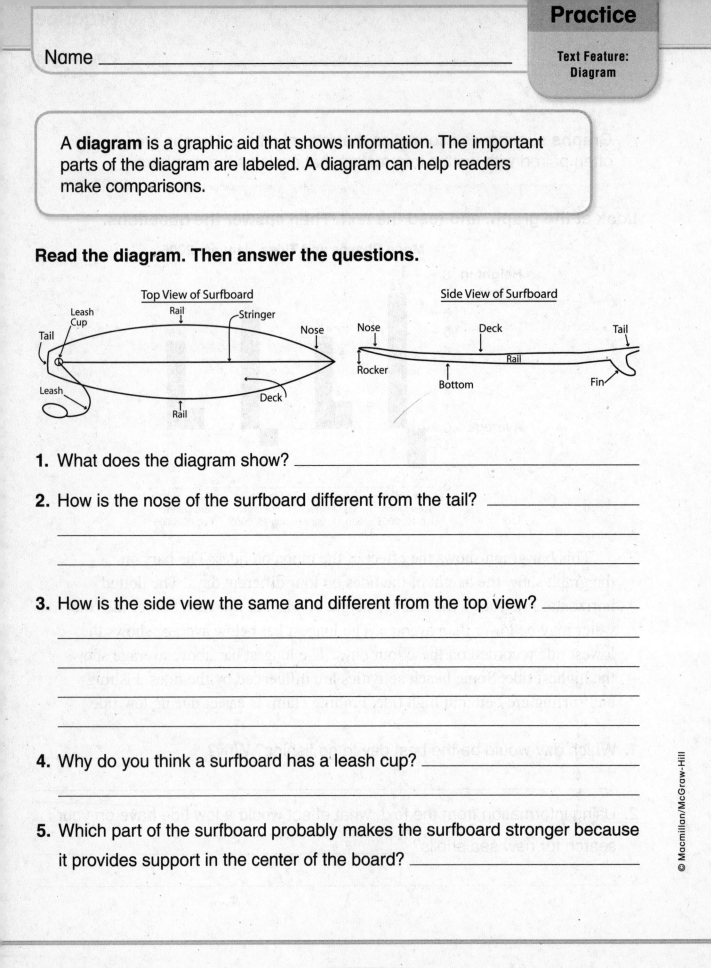

1. What does the diagram show? _____

2. How is the nose of the surfboard different from the tail? _____
   _____
   _____

3. How is the side view the same and different from the top view? _____
   _____
   _____
   _____
   _____

4. Why do you think a surfboard has a leash cup? _____
   _____

5. Which part of the surfboard probably makes the surfboard stronger because
   it provides support in the center of the board? _____

Suffixes are word parts that are often derived from Greek, Latin, and other languages. They are added to the ends of base words to change their meanings or their parts of speech.

- The suffix *-ity* means "the state of." For example, when you add the suffix *-ity* to *visible*, the word *visibility* means "the state of being visible."
- The suffix *-ion* means "act or process." When you add *-ion* to *demonstrate*, the word *demonstration* means "the act of demonstrating."
- The suffix *-ous* means "having the qualities of." For example, when you add *-ous* to the word *poison*, the word *poisonous* means "having the qualities of poison."

**In each sentence, underline the word that includes the suffix
-ity, *-ion*, or *-ous*. Then write each word and its meaning. Remember
that there may be spelling changes when you add the suffix.**

1. The mischievous girl liked to play tricks on her sisters.

_____

2. Amalia has the ability to make friends easily.

_____

3. With no hesitation, the boy loudly declared, "I want to go, too!"

_____

4. Juan was suspicious of his younger brother when the last cookie
disappeared.

_____

5. Our Spanish teacher always makes us work on our pronunciation.

_____

Name _____

A. Reading Strategy: Set a Purpose for Reading

As you read, think about your purpose for reading. You might set your own purpose for reading, or your teacher might set a purpose for you. Choose a text that you will read this week, and complete the activity.

Look at the title. What do you think the text will be about? _____

_____

_____

Look at any pictures or photographs that go with the text. What do they tell you about the topic? _____

_____

_____

Read the first paragraph. Why do you think the author wrote the text? _____

_____

_____

Think about your answers to the first three questions. What is your purpose for reading this text? _____

B. Independent Reading Log

Choose something you would like to read. After reading, complete the reading log. Be sure to paraphrase, or tell the main idea or meaning of the text. Keep the details or events in the correct order. You may use the log to talk to others about what you read.

Genre _____

Title _____

Author _____

This Text Is About _____

_____

_____

© Macmillan/McGraw-Hill

Name _____

The letters **ur**, **er**, **ir**, and **ear** can stand for the **/ûr/** sound, as in **fur**, **her**, **bird**, and **earn**. The letters **ear** and **eer** can stand for the **/îr/** sound, as in **fear** and **deer**.

A. Place each word in the column that best represents its vowel sound.

squirm   dreary   engineer   verse   clear
nerve   lurch   learn   sneer   ear

/ûr/, as in *fur*	/îr/, as in *fear*
1. _____	6. _____
2. _____	7. _____
3. _____	8. _____
4. _____	9. _____
5. _____	10. _____

B. Answer the questions using the chart above.

11. How can the /ûr/ sound be spelled?

_____

12. How can the /îr/ sound be spelled?

_____

Name _____

A. Read each word in Column 1. Match it with its definition in Column 2. Write the letter of the correct definition on the line next to each vocabulary word.

patriots	governor	navigation	stark
instruct	tyrant	inspect	

Column 1

1. tyrant ____
2. patriots ____
3. inspect ____
4. instruct ____
5. navigation ____
6. governor ____
7. stark ____

Column 2

a. to look at closely
b. cruel leader
c. a ship's course or position
d. those loyal to their country
e. harsh and grim
f. to teach
g. ruler or elected official

B. Complete the sentence with the correct word.

8. Paul Revere and his friends were (tyrants/patriots) _____ and helped protect the colonies.

9. The barren field looked (stark/inspect) _____.

10. Paul Revere tried to (inspect/instruct) _____ the colonists to prepare for war.

11. The (governor/tyrant) _____ ruled the colony in a fair manner.

As you read, you can **draw conclusions** by thinking about text clues and what you already know that connects to the text. This helps you arrive at a new understanding about the **characters and plot development** in a story.

Read the following lines from "The Midnight Ride of Paul Revere." Then answer the questions.

You know the rest in the books you have read
How the British Regulars fired and fled,
How the farmers gave them ball for ball,
From behind each fence and the farmyard wall,
Chasing the red-coats down the lane,
Then crossing the fields to emerge again
Under the trees at the turn of the road,
And only pausing to fire and load.

1. What conclusion can you make about the colonists fighting the British Regulars? What evidence supports your conclusion?

   _____

   _____

   _____

   _____

2. Did the British retreat? What line(s) from the poem support your conclusion?

   _____

3. How do you know that the colonists were determined to gain their independence? What was the result of their fight for freedom?

   _____

   _____

   _____

As you read *Sleds on Boston Common*, fill in the Conclusions Chart.

Text Clues	Conclusion

How does the information you wrote in the Conclusions Chart help you summarize *Sleds on Boston Common*?

As I read, I will pay attention to phrasing.

	Life in the colonies was changing. Roads had been built
10	connecting the cities. The colonies were trading with one
19	another more. People and ideas were moving along with
28	goods. These changes had made the ties among the colonists
38	stronger. They were beginning to feel more American
46	than British.
48	Then, in 1765, the British passed the Stamp Act. It was
58	one of the taxes that the British were using to help pay for
71	their war with France.
75	The colonists were furious. It wasn't only the money,
84	although times were hard. They were angry because they
93	hadn't voted for this tax. The colonists believed that only
103	representatives they chose could ask them to pay taxes.
111	The colonists said there could be "no taxation without
121	representation."
122	And so the first step toward the American Revolution
131	began over a fight about taxes.
137	Colonists refused to pay the stamp tax. Some people
146	boycotted, or refused to buy, British goods or enter any store
157	that carried British goods. 161

Comprehension Check

1. What caused the colonists to feel more American than British?
Cause and Effect

2. Why were colonists so angry about the Stamp Act? **Main Idea and Details**

	Words Read	–	Number of Errors	=	Words Correct Score
First Read		–		=	
Second Read		–		=	

As you read, you draw conclusions by combining clues in the text with what you know. Authors may give text clues in the form of **sensory details**. Sensory details appeal to your five senses, helping you see, hear, taste, smell, and feel parts of the story. These details help bring the story to life. You can use a thesaurus to find alternate words choices for words in texts.

Read the passage below. Then answer the questions that follow.

The smiling children shuffled quickly into the chilly yellow school bus. Mr. Shintoy barked out their names and marked his list. "Thanks for being quiet while I checked names. Everyone is here. You can visit with your neighbor while we ride to the lab." As the bus bounced down the road in the morning sun, voices rose with excitement about the experiments the children would do that day.

1. What conclusion can you draw about what is happening in the passage?

   _____

2. List sensory clues in the story that help you draw conclusions about what is

   happening. _____

   _____

   _____

3. List clues from your own experience that help you draw conclusions about

   the passage: _____

   _____

4. List words from a thesaurus that could be alternate choices for the following
   words from the story:

   children _____   neighbor _____

   shuffled _____   bounced _____

   quickly _____   experiments _____

   barked _____   do _____

Name _____

Narrative poetry is poetry that tells a story or gives an account of events. **Meter** is the regular arrangement of accented and unaccented syllables in a line of poetry. **Alliteration** is the repetition of the same initial consonant sounds in a series of words.

A. Read the passage from the poem. Mark the meter of each line by separating the syllables with a slash. Then underline the accented syllables. Then answer the questions.

> Meanwhile, his friend, through alley and street,
> Wanders and watches, with eager ears,
> Till in the silence around him he hears
> The muster of men at the barrack door,
> And the measured tread of the grenadiers,
> Marching down to their boats on the shore.

1. Based on this passage, how do you know the poem is narrative poetry?

   _____

   _____

   _____

2. Which lines use alliteration? Give examples.

   _____

   _____

   _____

   _____

B. Rewrite the following line so that it uses alliteration.

3. Marching down to their boats on the shore.

   _____

Many long words have smaller base words within them. With many words it is easy to build **word families** by adding a **suffix** or a **prefix** to a base word.

A. For the words listed below, write an additional word that belongs to the same word family.

1. patriot

unpatriotic _____

2. tyrant

tyrannical _____

3. navigate

navigation _____

4. govern

governor _____

B. Complete the sentence by using the correct word from the word families above.

5. The American colonists created their own _____.

6. A person who is not loyal to his or her country is said to be

_____.

7. Paul Revere showed great _____ for the American colonies during his midnight ride.

8. The _____ of the *Somerset*, a British ship, had to have good eyesight.

A. Reading Strategy: Set a Purpose for Reading

As you read, think about your purpose for reading. You might set your own purpose for reading, or your teacher might set a purpose for you. Choose a text that you will read this week, and complete the activity.

Study the chart. Then complete the statements.

Genre	Possible Purposes for Reading
Fiction/Drama/Poetry	to be entertained, to think about a topic in a new way, to understand something about life or people
Informational Text	to learn about a topic, to learn how to do something
Persuasive Text	to learn about a topic, to form an opinion about something, to decide whether to take an action

The genre that I will read is _____.

The subject of the text is _____.

My purpose for reading is to _____.

B. Independent Reading Log

Choose something you would like to read. After reading, complete the reading log. Be sure to paraphrase, or tell the main idea or meaning of the text. Keep the details or events in the correct order. You may use the log to talk to others about what you read.

Genre _____

Title _____

Author _____

This Text Is About _____

_____

_____

Name _____

- The **/ô/** sound can be spelled **aw**, as in **law**, **au**, as in **haul**, **ough**, as in **bought** or **augh**, as in **taught**.

- The **/ou/** sound can be spelled **ou**, as in **counter**, or **ow**, as in **cow**.

- The **/oi/** sound can be spelled **oi**, as in **boil**, or **oy**, as in **loyal**.

Write the words below in the correct column according to their vowel sounds. Remember that different letters can make the same vowel sounds. Circle the letters in each word that make the /ô/, /ou/, or /oi/ vowel sound.

dawdle	brought	crowd	toil	sought
joint	loyal	noise	mountain	loud
daughter	fountain	sprawls	foil	point
house	thought	bawl	royal	town

/ô/ sound, as in *law*	/ou/ sound, as in *now*	/oi/ sound, as in *boy*
1. _____	1. _____	1. _____
2. _____	2. _____	2. _____
3. _____	3. _____	3. _____
4. _____	4. _____	4. _____
5. _____	5. _____	5. _____
6. _____	6. _____	6. _____
7. _____	7. _____	7. _____

| specimens | transferred | murky | dormant |
| biology | scoured | research | observer |

Choose the word that best replaces the underlined word or words. Then write the word on the line.

1. If you are curious about <u>the study of living things,</u> you can make amazing discoveries. _____

2. First you must become <u>someone who watches everything around you.</u>

   _____

3. Your <u>investigations</u> might take you to a park or even to a lake, where you can study life under the water. _____

4. Sometimes a lake will look <u>as though it has no activity,</u> but it is really filled with life. _____

5. In the water you may find minerals to be <u>cleaned</u> back in the lab.

   _____

6. Even if the water is <u>thick and dark,</u> you will probably find something fascinating. _____

7. Take <u>samples</u> of the water so that you can study them under a microscope.

   _____

8. After you have <u>moved</u> the samples to a slide, you can examine them.

   _____

Events in a story or steps in an experiment usually happen in chronological order. If you can recognize and follow the **sequence**, you will better understand when important events happen and how they relate to each other. Words such as *first*, *then*, *next*, *now*, *when*, *before*, *after*, and *finally* help signal the order in which events or steps occur.

Read the scientific method. Label each step of the scientific method below.

   Scientific method is specific steps scientists take during an experiment. Scientists try to answer questions they have by performing several tests. By following a specific sequence during different experiments, they are able to determine the answers to their questions.

1. **Initial or First Observation:** Scientists notice something and wonder why.
2. **Gather Information:** Scientists try to find out more.
3. **Hypothesis:** Scientists take their initial observation and create a question that can be tested. A hypothesis should make a prediction of the outcome.
4. **Testing:** Scientists will perform experiments and record data.
5. **Draw a Conclusion:** Using the information from their tests, scientists will compare this data to their hypothesis to see if their prediction is correct or not.

1. Finally I conclude my hypothesis was correct. The birds made a nest to hold their eggs. _____

2. Then I learned more from a book about birds laying eggs in the spring.

   _____

3. First I see two blue birds. One is flying from tree to tree. The other is gathering twigs. It is springtime. _____

4. Next I observe the birds for a week. They choose a large tree branch. The birds gather more twigs and start building a nest. I see three bird eggs.

   _____

5. I predict the birds will make a nest to hold their eggs.

   _____

© Macmillan/McGraw-Hill

Name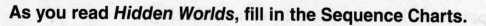

As you read *Hidden Worlds*, fill in the Sequence Charts.

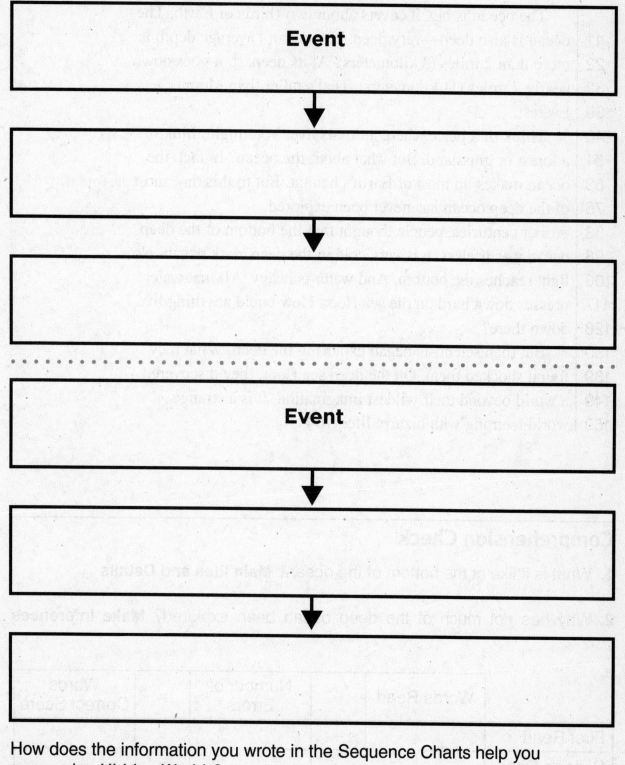

Event

↓

↓

Event

↓

↓

How does the information you wrote in the Sequence Charts help you summarize *Hidden Worlds*?

As I read, I will pay attention to expression and phrasing.

	The ocean is big. It covers about two-thirds of Earth. The
11	ocean is also deep—very deep. The ocean's average depth is
22	more than 2 miles (3 kilometers). At its deepest, it goes down
32	nearly 7 miles (11 kilometers). That's taller than Mount
39	Everest.
40	Think of a place where animals live. You might think of
51	a forest or grassland. But what about the ocean? In fact, the
63	ocean makes up most of Earth's habitat. But to this day, most
75	of the deep ocean has never been explored.
83	For centuries, people thought that the bottom of the deep
93	ocean was lifeless. It is very cold in the deep, dark ocean. No
106	light reaches the bottom. And water is heavy. All that water
117	presses down hard on the sea floor. How could anything live
128	down there?
130	But then scientists began exploring the deep. What they
139	found shocked them. On the deep sea floor, they discovered
149	a world beyond their wildest imagination. It is a strange
159	world teeming with bizarre life. 164

Comprehension Check

1. What is it like at the bottom of the ocean? **Main Idea and Details**

2. Why has not much of the deep ocean been explored? **Make Inferences**

	Words Read	–	Number of Errors	=	Words Correct Score
First Read		–		=	
Second Read		–		=	

Writers use different organizational patterns to present information. The subject, as well as the purpose for writing, helps the writer decide which pattern to use. Here are several common patterns:
Sequential order: uses chronological order, or time order, to show what happened or to show the steps in a process
Cause-and-effect: presents an event and what led to it or what happened because of it
Compare-and-contrast: shows how two things or ideas are alike and different
Classification schemes: groups things or ideas according to shared qualities

Read each passage. Then answer the questions that follow.

Follow these steps when you do science experiments. First, read and understand the directions. Next, talk with your teacher and lab partners. Gather the items you will need for the experiment. Do the work, and then clean up your work area. Finally, write up the results.

1. Which organizational pattern did the writer use for this passage?

_____

2. Why would the writer choose this pattern?

_____

Butterflies and moths look alike; however, there are ways to tell them apart. Butterfly wings usually are bright colors; moth wings look dull. A butterfly's body is thin and smooth. A moth's body is round and fuzzy. Butterflies are out during the day, but moths are out at night.

3. Which organizational pattern did the writer use for this passage?

_____

4. Why would the writer choose this pattern?

_____

When you read poetry, pay attention to the poem's **rhyme scheme** and **rhythm**. The rhyme scheme is a pattern of words that have the same ending sound, such as *light* and *tight*. Rhythm is the regular repetition of accented or stressed syllables in the lines of a poem. Rhythm gives the poem a steady beat, almost like that of music.

A. In the poem below, fill in the blanks by choosing a word from the list that completes the rhyme scheme. Write the word on the lines provided.

right	round	glow	roar

1. We're in the rocket, set to go.

   The lift-off lights begin to _____.

2. The engines rumble, then they _____.

   Can we still run right out the door?

3. The spacecraft rolls from left to _____.

   And soon we rocket out of sight.

4. But wait! It's over. We're all safe and sound.

   Oh, it was just the simulator spinning _____.

B. Identify the rhythm in these lines of the poem. Underline the accented syllables.

   The spacecraft rolls from left to right.
   And soon we rocket out of sight.
   But wait! It's over. We're all safe and sound.
   Oh, it was just the simulator spinning round.

Many words in English have **roots** from ancient **Greek, Latin,** or other languages. Sometimes Latin or Greek word parts create a word family, or a group of words with a common feature or pattern. For example, the Greek root *geo* means "earth." The words *geography, geology, geographer, geode, geometry,* and *geometric* form a word family based on the words' Greek root *geo*.

Origin	Greek	Latin	Greek	Latin	Latin
Word part	bio	dict	tele	man	terr
Meaning	life	speak	far away	hand	earth

Look at the Latin and Greek word parts above. Choose the word in parentheses that best fits with the other two words to form a word family. Then write the word on the line.

1. bionic   biography   (biosphere/bicker)   _____

2. dictate   dictation   (dice/dictionary)   _____

3. telethon   telephone   (telescope/territory)   _____

4. manner   maneuver   (manicure/main)   _____

5. diction   dictator   (decorate/edict)   _____

6. manual   manufacture   (manuscript/mane)   _____

7. terrarium   terrestrial   (terrible/terrace)   _____

8. television   telegram   (telecast/teller)   _____

9. biology   biologist   (bisect/biographer)   _____

10. telescopic   telepathy   (telegraph/tale)   _____

A. Reading Strategy: Ask Questions

Asking questions can help you understand what you read. Some questions help you think about what a text says. Choose a text that you are reading this week, and complete the activity.

Use the chart to find questions you can ask about the text. Then fill in the blanks to ask and answer questions about the text.

	Fiction/Drama	Poetry	Biography/ Autobiography	Informational/ Persuasive Text
What does the text say about . . .	a character's thoughts, words, or actions; events that take place; the setting	the poem's subject, the speaker's feelings or actions	the subject's thoughts, words, or actions; events that take place	the text's topic, events that take place, causes and effects, problems and solutions, the author's views

Question: What does the text say about _____?

Answer: _____

Question: What does the text say about _____?

Answer: _____

B. Independent Reading Log

Choose something you would like to read. After reading, complete the reading log. Be sure to paraphrase, or tell the main idea or meaning of the text. Keep the details or events in the correct order. You may use the log to talk to others about what you read.

Genre _____

Title _____

Author _____

This Text Is About _____

_____

_____

Name _____

Add the letter **s** to most words to make them plural. Add **-es** to words that end in **s**, **x**, **z**, **ch**, or **sh** to form plurals. For example, **bunch** becomes **bunches**. When a word ends in the letter **y** and has a consonant before the **y**, change the **y** to **i** and then add **-es**. For example, the plural form of **bunny** is **bunnies**.

A. Write the plural form of each word on the line provided.

1. risk _____

2. century _____

3. compass _____

4. ability _____

5. rattler _____

6. loss _____

7. academy _____

8. tax _____

B. Look at each plural word below. Then write the singular form of the word on the line provided.

9. tongues _____

10. pouches _____

11. babies _____

12. forests _____

13. stories _____

14. branches _____

15. dictionaries _____

A. From each pair of words below, circle the word that best completes the sentence. Then write the correct word on the line provided.

1. Snakes are (predators/reptiles) because they live by hunting and eating other animals. _____

2. There are about 30 (brands/species) of rattlesnake. _____

3. A rattler shakes its tail as a warning before (fleeing/lunging) toward you.

   _____

4. You can (survive/avoid) a snake bite if you get help right away.

   _____

5. Snakes can feel another animal approaching because the ground (vibrates/twists). _____

6. Rattlesnakes often blend in with their (surroundings/forests), which makes them hard to see. _____

7. The hikers were (unprepared/alert) after rattlesnakes were spotted on the trail. _____

8. A rattlesnake shoots poison through its fangs when it bites its (prey/venom). _____

B. Write new sentences for two of the vocabulary words used above. Then underline the vocabulary word.

9. _____

   _____

10. _____

    _____

> The **main idea** is what all of the **details** in a paragraph or passage have in common. It is what the text is mostly about. By recognizing the details, you will be able to determine the main idea.

The introductory paragraphs below come from *Rattlers!* Read the paragraphs and answer the questions.

Rattlesnakes have a bad reputation. No wonder! They look mean. They sound spooky. And you know about their nasty bite. But mostly they're misunderstood. So here is all you ever wanted to know about rattlesnakes.

They are a group of snakes that have what no other snakes have: rattle-tipped tails. They also have thick bodies, wide heads, cat-like eyes, and long, hollow fangs that fold away when they're not needed. Their dull colors and patchy patterns help them blend with their surroundings.

1. List three details about the characteristics of rattlesnakes that you identified in the text.

   a. _____

   _____

   b. _____

   _____

   c. _____

   _____

2. After reading the details, what do you think is the main idea of *Rattlers!*? Circle the letter of the correct main idea.

   a. Rattlesnakes are poisonous snakes that eat other animals.

   b. Rattlesnakes have a bad reputation because they are misunderstood.

   c. People must be brave to study rattlesnakes in the wild.

Name _____

As you read a section of *Rattlers!*, fill in the Main Idea and
Details Chart.

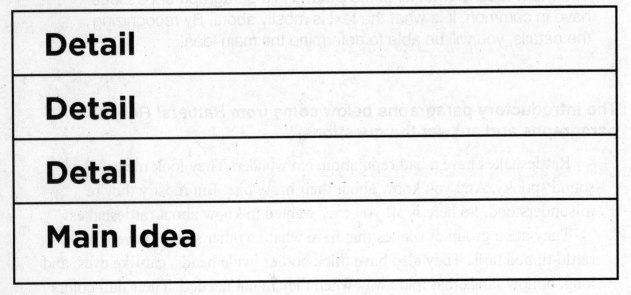

| Detail |
| Detail |
| Detail |
| Main Idea |

How does the information you wrote in this Main Idea and Details Chart
help you summarize the section of *Rattlers!*?

As you read a section of *Rare Rattler Rescue!*, fill in the Main Idea
and Details Chart.

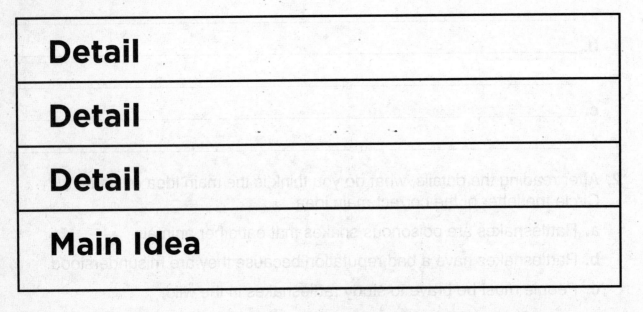

| Detail |
| Detail |
| Detail |
| Main Idea |

How does the information you wrote in this Main Idea and Details Chart
help you summarize the section of *Rare Rattler Rescue!*?

© Macmillan/McGraw-Hill

Name _____

As I read, I will pay attention to expression and phrasing.

11	Sea snakes live in the waters of the Indian and Pacific oceans. Since snakes are cold-blooded and depend on warmth
20	from their **surroundings**, their range is limited to the warm
30	tropics and nearby seas. Many live near coral reefs, those
40	stony underwater ridges that attract sea life of all kinds.
50	The total number of snake **species** is over 2,700. There are
61	only about 50 species of true sea snakes. But sea snakes may
73	be the most numerous of all snakes.
80	Most sea snakes are from two feet to a little more than
92	three feet long. A few grow to about eight feet. Most sea
104	snakes have slender bodies that help them move through the
114	water easily.
116	Living in the sea is a challenge for the sea snakes. They
128	have adapted to the sea in several ways. One way is through
140	their shape. 142

Comprehension Check

1. Why do sea snakes have to live in warm waters? **Main Idea and Details**

2. What is one way that sea snakes have adapted to living in water? **Main Idea and Details**

	Words Read	–	Number of Errors	=	Words Correct Score
First Read		–		=	
Second Read		–		=	

A myth presents a story about a culture's beliefs and traditions. One important kind of myth is an **origin myth**. Early people often explained natural phenomena or everyday occurrences that were difficult for them to understand by telling a story. For instance, the Greeks explained the movement of the sun by telling a story about a charioteer who pulled the sun across the sky. Many cultures have origin myths that tell about the beginning of Earth, the first people, and so on.

Read the origin myth below. Then answer the question.

When the world was very young, Zeus made Pandora, a beautiful woman. All of the gods gave her gifts, including beauty, charm, and lovely clothes. One of the gifts was a box, which was filled with evil things. It contained sickness, war, and sorrow. Pandora did not know what was in the box. She was told only that she should not open it.

Pandora was happy, but she always wondered what was in the box. One day, she could not wait any longer. She opened the box. Out flew all of the evils in the world. Pandora tried to snap the lid shut, but she was too late. The only thing that she could keep in the box was hope. This is why, even when the world is full of problems, people still have hope.

What phenomenon or occurrence is explained in this origin myth?

_____

_____

_____

Legends are stories that come down from the past and are based on the traditions of a people or region. The **hero** is the main character in a legend, who often does something brave to help others. **Personification** is the assignment of human characteristics to an animal, a thing, or an idea.

Read the following passage from "How Poison Came into the World." Answer the questions on the lines provided.

Long ago, when the Earth was young, the Choctaw people loved to swim in the cool waters of the bayou. But the Choctaw had to be very careful when swimming, because a poisonous plant grew in the heart of the bayou. This plant lived below the surface of the water, so swimmers could not see it until it was too late.

The plant, however, did not want to hurt his friends the Choctaw. As more people fell ill, the poor plant became sadder and sadder. Finally, he decided to give away his poison. The plant called the chiefs of the wasps and snakes to meet with him. He asked them to take his poison.

1. Who is the hero in "How Poison Came into the World"? Explain your answer.

_____

_____

2. How is the plant personified? _____

_____

3. How does the legend reflect a certain region or people? _____

_____

4. What sacrifice do you think the plant will make? _____

_____

5. What is the point of this legend? _____

_____

Name _____

> **Context clues** restate what other words mean.
> As you read, you can use context clues to help you define
> unfamiliar words.

**Look for context clues to help you define the underlined word in
each sentence. Then write the meaning of the underlined word on
the line provided.**

1. Many <u>species</u>, or kinds, of rattlesnake are found in the United States.

   _____

2. A rattlesnake shoots <u>venom</u>, or poison, through its fangs when it bites.

   _____

3. Rattlers blend in with their <u>surroundings</u> because their dull colors and

   patchy skin match their environment. _____

4. The fangs of a rattlesnake fold away when they're <u>unnecessary</u>, or not

   needed. _____

5. Rattlesnakes use <u>pits</u>, or dents, on their heads to sense the body heat of

   other animals. _____

6. When a rattlesnake shakes its tail, the rattle <u>vibrates</u> and makes noise.

   _____

7. Snakes can move quickly, even though they just <u>slither</u>, or slide, along.

   _____

8. Some animals are not <u>bothered</u>, or harmed, by rattlesnake venom.

   _____

© Macmillan/McGraw-Hill

Name _____

A. Reading Strategy: Ask Questions

Asking questions can help you understand what you read. Some
questions help you think about what a text means. Choose a text that
you are reading this week, and complete the chart.

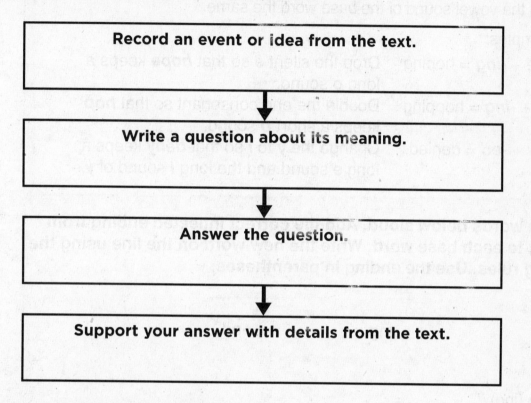

Record an event or idea from the text.

↓

Write a question about its meaning.

↓

Answer the question.

↓

Support your answer with details from the text.

B. Independent Reading Log

Choose something you would like to read. After reading, complete the
reading log. Be sure to paraphrase, or tell the main idea or meaning of
the text. Keep the details or events in the correct order. You may use the
log to talk to others about what you read.

Genre _____

Title _____

Author _____

This Text Is About _____

_____

_____

Name _____

Practice

Phonics/Word Study:
Inflectional Endings

An **inflectional ending** is an ending that is added to a word to show a change in the way the word is used. When you add an inflected ending, follow the spelling rules shown in the examples below to keep the vowel sound of the base word the same.

Examples:

hope + *-ing* = hoping	Drop the silent *e* so that **hope** keeps a long *o* sound.
hop + *-ing* = hopping	Double the end consonant so that **hop** keeps a short *o* sound.
deny + *-ed* = denied	Change the *y* to *i* so that **deny** keeps a long *e* sound and the long *i* sound of *y*.

Say the words below aloud. Add the correct inflected ending from the box to each base word. Write the new word on the line using the spelling rules. Use the ending in parentheses.

```
    -ing              -ed
```

1. drip (ing)   =   _____

2. amuse (ing)   =   _____

3. jog (ing)   =   _____

4. qualify (ed)   =   _____

5. rake (ing)   =   _____

6. rely (ed)   =   _____

7. forbid (ing)   =   _____

8. ease (ing)   =   _____

9. apply (ed)   =   _____

10. regret (ed)   =   _____

| observed | inhibit | investigating |
| conquer | insight | |

A. Complete each sentence by choosing the best word from the box.

1. One doctor is _____ how diseases spread among students at school.

2. She has _____ hundreds of students in the classroom.

3. She believes that getting plenty of sleep can _____ illnesses.

4. This _____ might help students stay healthy.

5. Studies like this are helping to _____ disease.

B. Choose three vocabulary words. Write a sentence of your own for each of these words.

6. _____

_____

7. _____

_____

8. _____

_____

Understanding an **author's purpose** for writing helps readers evaluate the text they are reading. Authors may be presenting information about a topic, writing to entertain, or trying to persuade readers about an issue. Identifying an author's purpose can help readers choose an appropriate reading strategy. Readers may decide to read informational pieces more carefully than a story that merely entertains.

Read the passage, and answer the questions.

Penguins live in the Southern Hemisphere. Most penguins live in places far from people. Some live on the southern tip of South America. Some live on islands in the Pacific Ocean. A few build nests in Antarctica.

There are 17 species of penguins. The Little Blue Penguin is the smallest species. It weighs about two pounds. The largest species, the Emperor Penguin, can weigh up to 80 pounds. Although they look different in some ways, all penguins share certain features. They all are covered with feathers, are warm-blooded, and have webbed feet. Like all birds, penguins have wings. However, penguins never fly. Instead, they use their flipper-like wings to dive deep beneath the water.

1. What is the author's purpose in this passage?

_____

2. Write a statement from the passage that helped you to determine the author's purpose.

_____

_____

3. Do you think the author accomplished his or her purpose with this passage? Why or why not?

_____

_____

© Macmillan/McGraw-Hill

As you read *These Robots Are Wild!*, fill in the Author's Purpose Chart.

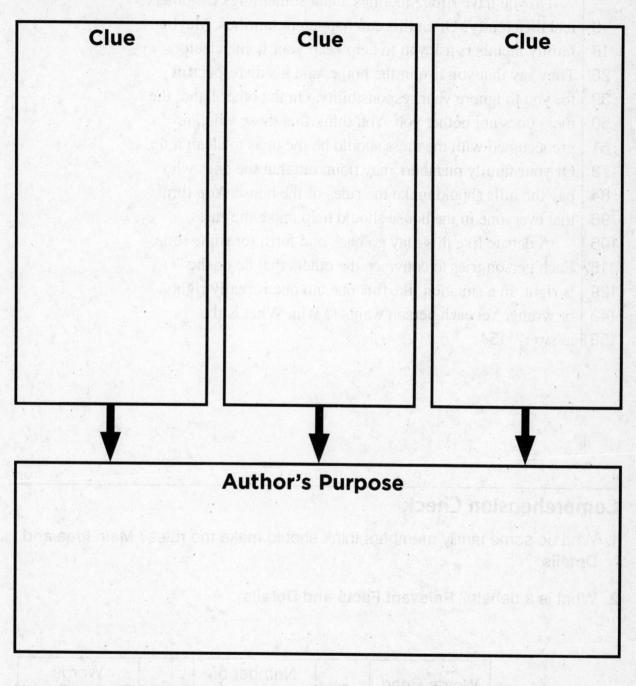

Clue	Clue	Clue

Author's Purpose

How does the information you wrote in the Author's Purpose Chart help you monitor comprehension of *These Robots Are Wild!*?

© Macmillan/McGraw-Hill

These Robots Are Wild!
Grade 5/Unit 2

67

Name _____

As I read, I will pay attention to phrasing.

	Do you have strong feelings about something? Do others
9	feel differently? Often this can happen in families. Maybe
18	family members ask you to help keep your home clean.
28	They say that you live in the home, and it's disrespectful
39	for you to ignore your responsibility. On the other hand, the
50	mess does not bother you. You think that those who are
61	preoccupied with the mess should be the ones to clean it up.
73	Or your family members may point out that the ones who
84	pay the bills should make the rules of the house. You think
96	that everyone in the house should help make the rules.
106	A debate like this may go back and forth for some time.
118	Each person tries to convince the others that he or she
129	is right. In a situation like this one, no one is really right
142	or wrong. Yet each person wants to win. What is the
153	answer? 154

Comprehension Check

1. Who do some family members think should make the rules? **Main Idea and Details**

2. What is a debate? **Relevant Facts and Details**

	Words Read	–	Number of Errors	=	Words Correct Score
First Read		–		=	
Second Read		–		=	

Name _____

An alert reader can identify an author's viewpoint and explain the basic relationships among ideas by examining three writing devices:
Parallelism: repeating words, phrases, or grammatical structures to make a point; for example, "Just as *this is true*, so must *that be true*."
Comparison: showing how two things are alike; for example, "The new robots are like insects because they can get into small places."
Causality: showing how one thing leads to another; for example, "If we can find out how insects move, then we can build better robots."

Read the passage. Then fill in the chart and answer the question.

Just as we explore space, we should explore small things in nature. For example, insects can help us solve problems. Humans are like insects because we need food, water, and air. However, insects live easily in places where humans do not. If we can find out how insects learn to live in different places, then we may learn to live on other planets. We should discover, use, and appreciate these small things. If we can learn all there is to know about insects, then we will be wiser.

Sentence from Passage	Device	What It Shows
Just as we explore space, we should explore small things in nature.		
Humans are like insects because we need food, water, and air.		
If we can learn all there is to know about insects, then we will be wiser.		

What viewpoint does the author present in this argument? _____
_____

© Macmillan/McGraw-Hill

Name _____

A **library** often holds more than collections of books and magazines. Due to advances in technology, information can be stored and presented in many different forms. To use a library or **media center** successfully, choose the correct resources.

Choose the resource from the chart that would provide useful information for each item below. Write the name of the resource on the line provided.

Sample of Media Center Resources
Thomas Pakenham's book of photographs about trees around the world
online encyclopedia, key words "wildfire" and "containment"
CD entitled *The Music of the Brazilian Rain Forest*
video documentary called *Three Forest Biomes and the Animals That Live in Them*
print encyclopedia, volume B, article about common trees
CD-ROM entitled *Maps, Geography, and the Environment*

1. Which resource would you use to read articles about these common trees in the United States: black cherry, box elder, black willow?

   _____

2. Which resource would you use to hear what a typical day in a rain forest sounds like? _____

   _____

3. Which resource would you use to find pictures of a tree named "General Sherman" in California and a tree called a "dancing lime" in Germany? _____

   _____

4. Which resource would you use to learn about techniques used to control wildfires? _____

   _____

© Macmillan/McGraw-Hill

The root of a word is the part that carries its main meaning. The roots of many English words originally came from Greek, Latin, or other languages. Knowing **Greek and Latin roots** can help you figure out the meaning of unfamiliar words.

Root	Meaning	Language
astr	star	Greek
chron	time	Greek
gen	birth	Greek
sci	know	Latin
san	health	Latin
aud	hear	Latin

Use the chart above to help you choose the word in parentheses that is being described.

1. This is a noun that means "the time order in which events occur." (chronology, covert) _____

2. This is the study of the history of births in families. (pharmacology, genealogy) _____

3. This is a large building or room where people listen to concerts. (auditorium, concerto) _____

4. This adjective means "awake and able to think and know." (conscious, determined) _____

5. This adjective means "free from germs that cause illness." (laundered, sanitary) _____

6. This is the study of objects in space. (anthropology, astronomy)

_____

A. Reading Strategy: Ask Questions

Asking questions can help you understand what you read. Some questions help you think about how well a text is written. Choose a text that you are reading this week, and complete the activity.

Ask and answer questions about the purpose of the text.

1. Why was the text written? _____

_____

2. How well do events or ideas in the text help it meet that purpose?

_____

_____

_____

Ask and answer questions about the author's message.

3. What is the author's message? _____

_____

4. How well do events or ideas in the text help the author express that

message? _____

_____

_____

B. Independent Reading Log

Choose something you would like to read. After reading, complete the reading log. Be sure to paraphrase, or tell the main idea or meaning of the text. Keep the details or events in the correct order. You may use the log to talk to others about what you read.

Genre _____

Title _____

Author _____

This Text Is About _____

_____

A **contraction** is a shortened form of two words. An apostrophe
takes the place of the missing letters.
she is = she's   he will = he'll

A. Write the words each contraction stands for.

1. shouldn't _____

2. don't _____

3. you're _____

4. he's _____

5. won't _____

**B. Write the contraction that takes the place of the underlined
words.**

6. Sue <u>could not</u> decide which book to check out from the library.

_____

7. <u>She had</u> read a mystery last week. _____

8. She <u>did not</u> want to read a nonfiction book. _____

9. "I think <u>I will</u> read a tall tale about Sluefoot Sue," she decided.

_____

10. "<u>It will</u> be fun to read about a character who shares my name."

_____

launched	particles	dense	inflate
anchored	hydrogen	scientific	companion

A. Choose the word from the list above that best completes each sentence. Then write the word on the line.

1. The hot-air balloon soared through the air because it was not

   _____, or held down, to the ground by anything.

2. The balloons soar because the hot air is light and the air surrounding

   it is heavy and _____ .

3. People in hot-air balloons are _____ into the sky.

4. The large balloons _____ when they are filled with hot air.

5. The small pieces of matter in air move faster as the air heats. Then the

   _____ spread out, and the balloon rises.

6. Balloons filled with _____ float, because the gas is lighter
   than air.

7. Some people ride in hot-air balloons to do _____ experiments.

8. You and a _____ might enjoy sharing a hot-air balloon ride.

B. Label each statement *True* or *False*.

9. The science club launched the balloon, and it dug deep into the earth.

   _____

10. You can inflate a balloon with hydrogen or hot air. _____

11. The balloon will not move when it is anchored to the ground.

    _____

12. To conduct scientific experiments you must bring a companion.

    _____

A **fact** is a statement that can be proven true. An opinion is someone's personal feelings or beliefs about a subject. Opinions are not necessarily true or false. Facts can be verified by checking reliable sources.

A. Circle the letter of the correct answer to the following questions.

1. Which of the following statements is an opinion?

   a. All useful inventions are inspired by nature.

   b. Velcro was inspired by burrs that were stuck to George de Mestral's dog.

   c. It took eight years to perfect the design for Velcro.

2. Read the information about Thomas Edison and Alexander Graham Bell. Then choose the fact that can be concluded from the sentences.

   As a child, Thomas Edison asked a lot of questions. Alexander Graham Bell was already inventing by age 14.

   a. Thomas Edison asked too many questions.

   b. Few inventors are curious as children.

   c. Both inventors were curious children.

B. Write whether the statements below are facts or opinions.

3. Research has led to artificial limbs that can help people walk.

   _____

4. It took too long to develop the machine that produces cellophane.

   _____

Name _____

As you read _Up in the Air: The Story of Balloon Flight_, fill in the Fact and Opinion Chart.

Fact	Opinion

How does the information you wrote in the Fact and Opinion Chart help you monitor comprehension in _Up in the Air: The Story of Balloon Flight_?

Name _____

As I read, I will pay attention to rate and accuracy.

	It is a beautiful day at the football stadium. Fans fill the
12	seats and wait for the kickoff. Suddenly, a strange shadow
22	appears on the field. People sitting in the upper rows hear
33	a low whirring sound overhead. Floating in the sky is a
44	football-shaped balloon.
47	Most of us have seen them on television during sporting
57	events. They are like silent ships sailing on a sea of sky.
69	These strange-looking balloons are called blimps. They are
77	cousins to the hot-air balloon.
82	Blimps and hot-air balloons are part of a group of flying
93	machines known as lighter-than-air craft. They are filled
101	with gas that weighs less than air.
108	Blimps are also members of the airship family. Just like
118	boats, airships have motors and rudders. The motors give
127	airships speed. The rudders help steer. These additions make
136	airships very different from hot-air balloons. Hot-air balloons
144	have little control over their speed or direction. Airships can
154	even fly against the wind. 159

Comprehension Check

1. Compare and contrast blimps and hot-air balloons. **Compare and Contrast**

2. Where do people commonly see blimps? **Main Idea and Details**

	Words Read	–	Number of Errors	=	Words Correct Score
First Read		–		=	
Second Read		–		=	

Name _____

Informational writing often contains both facts and opinions. A fact is
information that can be proved true. An **opinion** is a statement that
cannot be proved. A reader should determine which statements are
facts and **verify** them by checking their accuracy in an encyclopedia
or another reliable source. Sometimes a writer will include
contradictory statements that disagree with each another. When
this happens, the reader needs to do additional checking.

Read the passage below. Then answer the questions that follow.

I felt like the luckiest kid in the world. I had won a contest by writing a
song for an ad for a hot air balloon company. My prize was a ride for two in
a hot air balloon! I took along my father as my guest.

We scheduled the ride for a Saturday morning. We took off from a field
near Austin. The balloon was above us, and the city was beneath us. Every
few moments, the burner blasted more heat into the balloon. Before we got
too high, I could see people below waving at our rainbow-striped balloon.
My mother and I waved back.

As we rode, I thought about what we had learned about balloons. I knew
that they had been invented in France over 200 years ago. People had been
enjoying this kind of ride for centuries!

All too soon, the ride was over. Our checkered flying machine came to
a rest outside town. I'll never forget that wonderful Friday morning!

1. List three contradictions in the passage. _____

_____

_____

_____

2. List two facts from the passage that you could verify in a book or on a

reliable Web site. _____

_____

_____

Name _____

When you read poetry, you often encounter poetic elements such as **similes** and **metaphors**. Similes and metaphors use language to create striking or unexpected images for the reader. These are figures of speech that compare or associate two things. Similes use *like* or *as* in the comparison. Metaphors compare without using *like* or *as*.

Read the poem to answer the following questions.

Balloon Flight Haiku

It floats in the air
like a bird's loosened feather,
drifting among blue.

The azure ocean
above our very heads
is where it sails high.

Unlike a feather,
it is guided by someone
who chooses its course.

1. What similes can you find in the haiku?

_____

2. What metaphors can you find in the haiku?

_____

3. What comparisons are made in the haiku?

_____

_____

4. Which comparison is not stated directly? How do you know the comparison is made?

_____

_____

Many English words have roots that originally came from the ancient Greek language. Knowing what the **Greek root** means will help you figure out the meaning of the word.

Root	Meaning
hydro	water
aster/astro	star
dem	people
graph	write
log/logue	word
pod	foot

Use the chart above to help you choose which word is being described in each item below.

1. The lightest gas, this element is found in water and all organic substances.

   (helium, hydrogen) _____

2. This is a noun that means "a conversation, often in a story."

   (dialogue, dialect) _____

3. This object has three "feet." (tricycle, tripod) _____

4. This kind of political system allows the people to vote for their government.

   (democracy, monarchy) _____

5. This is a form of communication that people use to write in Morse code.

   (telephone, telegraph) _____

6. This is the study of the stars and planets. (geology, astronomy)

   _____

A. Reading Strategy: Ask Questions

Asking questions can help you understand what you read. Some questions help you combine what you are reading with familiar ideas to improve your understanding. Choose a text that you are reading this week, determine its genre, and then complete the chart on a separate sheet of paper.

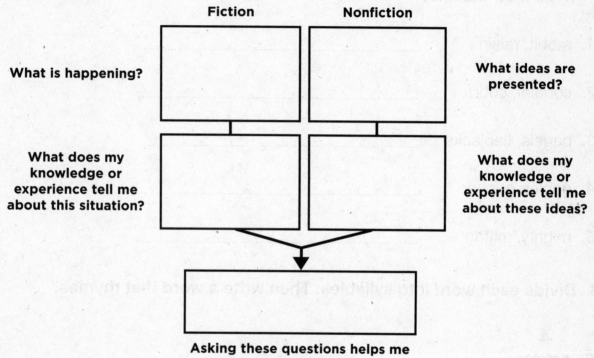

Fiction   Nonfiction

What is happening?   What ideas are presented?

What does my knowledge or experience tell me about this situation?   What does my knowledge or experience tell me about these ideas?

Asking these questions helps me understand...

B. Independent Reading Log

Choose something you would like to read. After reading, complete the reading log. Be sure to paraphrase, or tell the main idea or meaning of the text. Keep the details or events in the correct order. You may use the log to talk to others about what you read.

Genre _____

Title _____

Author _____

This Text Is About _____

_____

Name _____

A **closed syllable** ends in a consonant sound and usually has a short vowel sound.

A. Choose the word in each pair that has a closed first syllable. Write it on the line.

1. rabbit, raisin   _____

2. cobbler, cobra   _____

3. bagels, flapjacks   _____

4. goblet, gopher   _____

5. mighty, mitten   _____

B. Divide each word into syllables. Then write a word that rhymes.

6. splinter   _____

7. socket   _____

8. tunnel   _____

9. splendor   _____

10. mental   _____

Name _____

A. Select the correct word from the vocabulary words within the parentheses. Then write your choice on the line.

Hurricanes are tropical storms with rain and strong swirling winds.

Hurricanes form over the ocean where warm water is (available / beautiful)

_____ as a source of energy. The (property / atmosphere)

_____ surrounding a hurricane uses moisture from the

warm water to power the storm. When a hurricane moves toward land, a

(surge / destruction) _____ of water can cause flooding

in coastal areas. When a hurricane finally makes (waves / contact)

_____ with the land, high winds are a serious threat.

These powerful storms can cause much (destruction / atmosphere)

_____ to (surges / property) _____. The cost

of (contacts / damages) _____ from a hurricane can reach

billions of dollars.

B. Write your own paragraph about hurricanes, using at least three vocabulary words. Then underline each vocabulary word.

_____

_____

_____

_____

_____

_____

_____

Name _____

Description is an organizational pattern authors sometimes use to provide details about something. Signal words and phrases such as *most Important*, *for example*, *for instance*, or *to begin with* alert readers about an upcoming list or set of characteristics.

Read the paragraph. Then answer the questions below.

Hurricane Andrew was one of the worst hurricanes to hit the United States. Andrew first formed in the warm waters of the southern Atlantic Ocean in August 1992. To begin with, the storm had winds of only 40 miles per hour. As the storm continued to move over the warm ocean, it gained energy and grew stronger. When the wind speed reached 74 miles per hour, the storm was officially a hurricane and was named Andrew. Then Andrew's winds climbed to 155 miles per hour! Next, heavy rain moved onshore as Andrew made landfall in southern Florida. Seven inches of rain fell, and storm tides were as high as 17 feet. Hurricane Andrew caused significant destruction to property in the United States. Final damages eventually totaled $25 billion.

1. What is the first fact the author gives about the storm that became

   Hurricane Andrew? _____

   _____

2. What was the initial wind speed of the storm? _____

   _____

3. What signal word or phrase does the author use when describing Andrew's wind

   speed before it became a hurricane? _____

4. The author uses *next* to alert you to what descriptive fact? _____

   _____

5. What were the final damage costs? _____

   _____

Name _____

As you read _Hurricanes_, fill in the Description Chart.

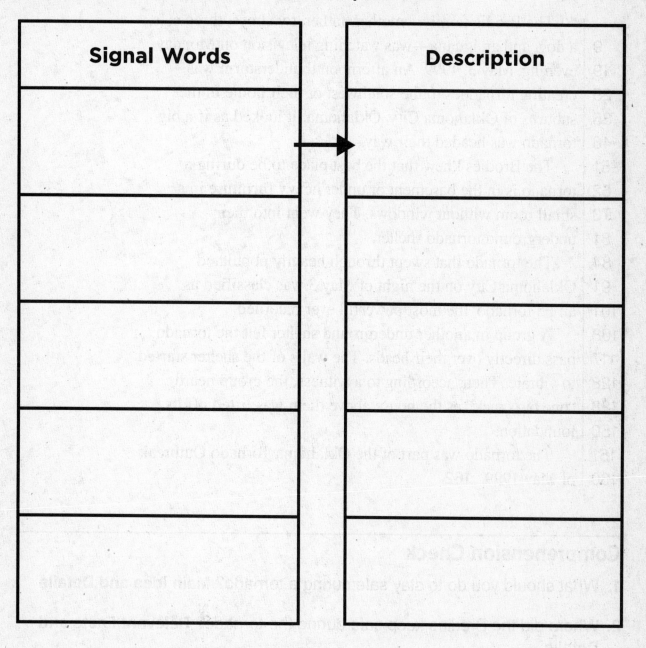

Signal Words	Description

How does the information you wrote in the Description Chart help you analyze the text structure of _Hurricanes_?

As I read, I will pay attention to expression and phrasing.

	The Brodie family—mother, father, two boys, three cats,
9	a dog, and an iguana—was watching television on Monday
19	evening, May 3, 1999. An afternoon thunderstorm was
25	creating tornadoes to the southwest of their home in the
35	suburbs of Oklahoma City, Oklahoma. It looked as if a big
46	tornado was headed their way.
51	The Brodies knew that the best place to be during a
62	tornado is in the basement or under heavy furniture in a
73	small room without windows. They went into their
81	underground tornado shelter.
84	The tornado that swept through heavily populated
91	Oklahoma City on the night of May 3 was classified as
101	an F5 tornado, the most powerful ever recorded.
108	A group in another underground shelter felt the tornado
117	pass directly over their heads. The walls of the shelter started
128	to vibrate. Then, according to a witness, the group heard
138	"one big crack" as the house above them was lifted off its
150	foundation.
151	The tornado was part of the Oklahoma Tornado Outbreak
160	of May 1999. 162

Comprehension Check

1. What should you do to stay safe during a tornado? **Main Idea and Details**

2. Where did the Brodies keep safe during the tornado? **Relevant Facts and Details**

	Words Read	–	Number of Errors	=	Words Correct Score
First Read		–		=	
Second Read		–		=	

Name _____

When reading persuasive texts, you may find statements that are
exaggerated, or made bigger or more important than they are.
Sometimes statements are **misleading**. They confuse readers
into thinking that something is true when it is not true. Misleading
statements also lead readers to expect something to be different
from what it really is.

Read the passage below. Then answer the questions that follow.

Gina, the weather reporter, stared at her computer. "We should be getting
a light dusting of snow, no excitement," Gina said. "It's the most boring
weather report since I was two years old."

"Too bad," the manager replied. "Why not make it sound more exciting so
that people will stay up to watch. Our ratings are low."

"I can't lie," Gina said. "Viewers will think I'm the world's biggest phony."

"It's not really lying to give the report a little 'twist' or to tell only part
of the story," the manager said. "People may think something different and
watch the show."

Later, as she was on camera giving the weather preview, Gina said, "Be
prepared for snow tomorrow! Will rush hour turn into your worst nightmare?
Will schools close? Stay tuned for the latest snow update!"

1. Underline two of Gina's statements that are exaggerations. Explain how you

   know that they are exaggerations. _____

   _____

   _____

2. Circle two of Gina's statements that are misleading. Explain why they are

   misleading. _____

   _____

   _____

   _____

Elements used in poetry include **personification**, or giving human characteristics to an animal, thing, or idea. Another element is **imagery**, or the use of descriptions to create vivid pictures in the reader's mind. An additional element is **onomatopoeia**, or the use of words that imitate the sounds of an object or action.

Read the poems and answer the questions.

Rabbit Mother sings her babies to sleep.
Tells them not to worry about the rain that splashes down,
Or that flash of lightning and sudden crash of thunder.
Her babies safe in a hillside burrow and Rabbit Mother taps her toes.
Waiting out another hurricane.

1. What literary devices does the poem above contain? How do you know?

_____

_____

2. What examples of onomatopoeia are used to describe the hurricane?

_____

Hurricane
Spinning leaves, flowing water.
All rotating together.
Like water spinning down the drain of an enormous bathtub.
Clockwise in the South. Counterclockwise in the North.
No toys, no bubbles.
Only wind and rain, and the hope that soon all will be safely dried
With the fluffy towel of sunshine.

3. What literary device does this poem have? How do you know?

_____

_____

_____

Name _____

Words with more than one meaning are **multiple-meaning words**. You can use context clues or other words in the sentence to help you figure out the most appropriate meaning. Sometimes you may need to consult a dictionary to find all the different meanings, parts of speech, pronunciation, and syllabication of the words.

Write a definition of the underlined word based on how it is used in the sentence.

1. When a hurricane's <u>eye</u> passes over you, the wind stops blowing.

   Eye means: _____

   _____

2. An <u>eye</u> will allow you to see your surroundings.

   Eye means: _____

   _____

3. Even during the worst of the storm, my mother maintained her <u>image</u> of calm.

   Image means: _____

   _____

4. The postcard had an <u>image</u> of a very famous painting on it.

   Image means: _____

   _____

5. A hurricane <u>watch</u> was issued, so we prepared to leave.

   Watch means: _____

   _____

6. My <u>watch</u> stopped keeping time because the battery died.

   Watch means: _____

   _____

A. Reading Strategy: Ask Questions

Asking questions can help you understand what you read. Choose a text that you are reading this week, and complete the activity.

1. Write a question about what the text says. _____

_____

2. Write a question about what the text means. _____

_____

3. Write a question about how well the text is written. _____

_____

4. Write a question that helps you combine what you are reading with familiar

ideas. _____

_____

5. Tell how asking and answering these questions helped you understand the

text. _____

_____

B. Independent Reading Log

Choose something you would like to read. After reading, complete the reading log. Be sure to paraphrase, or tell the main idea or meaning of the text. Keep the details or events in the correct order. You may use the log to talk to others about what you read.

Genre _____

Title _____

Author _____

This Text Is About _____

_____

The point where two syllables meet determines whether the vowel sound in the first syllable is long or short. A syllable that ends in a vowel (as in *hu-man*) is an **open syllable**. It has a **V/CV pattern,** and the vowel sound is long. A syllable that ends in a consonant (as in *wag-on*) is a closed syllable. It has a **VC/V pattern,** and the vowel sound is short.

Say the words below and break them into syllables. Then write the words in syllables on the lines provided. Write *long* if the word has a V/CV pattern. Write *short* if the word has a VC/V pattern.

1. humor _____ _____

2. pilot _____ _____

3. lemon _____ _____

4. punish _____ _____

5. lazy _____ _____

6. legal _____ _____

7. comet _____ _____

8. profile _____ _____

9. frozen _____ _____

10. proper _____ _____

11. waken _____ _____

12. tuna _____ _____

Name _____

appreciation	wares	treasurer	merchandise
educate	burdens	instruct	unfortunate

Replace the underlined word or words in each sentence with a word from the box.

1. The story of the fisher can <u>teach</u> readers about how people's greed can often get them in trouble. _____

2. The Market Club hired a <u>person who manages money</u> to help count all the money made at the market. _____

3. At the market, the basketmaker set out her <u>collection of goods</u> for all to see. _____

4. The fisher tricked others into leaving part of their <u>heavy loads</u> with him. _____

5. He tried to <u>direct</u> people to cross the river at the log. _____

6. Each person carefully carried his or her <u>products</u> across the log in order to reach the market. _____

7. He hoped that people would express their <u>gratitude</u> by paying him well. _____

8. The fisher's plan did not work, and he felt very <u>unlucky</u>. _____

© Macmillan/McGraw-Hill

Name _____

The **theme** of a story is the message that the author wants readers to understand. In a fable, the theme will often come in the form of a moral or lesson that the writer wants readers to apply to their own lives. This moral might be stated directly at the end of the fable. Sometimes though, the readers must figure out the moral theme by looking for clues in the story.

Read the summary of *The Catch of the Day*. Then answer the questions below.

A fisher decided to trick many people who were trying to get to the market. The fisher shook a log to convince each person it was unsafe to cross with so much merchandise. Finally, the ones who were tricked discovered what the fisher was up to and decided to trick him. As the fisher crossed the bridge, they shook the log so hard that he fell into the water. On the riverbank, the people the fisher tricked laughed and laughed. Later that day they ate a fine fish dinner!

1. What is the theme or moral lesson of this story?

_____

2. What are some clues about the moral that you found in the story?

_____

_____

3. What kind of traditional fable character is the fisher?

_____

4. How is the theme of *The Catch of the Day* like the theme of "Anansi and Common Sense"? How is it different?

_____

_____

_____

Name _____

As you read *The Catch of the Day*, fill in the Theme Chart.

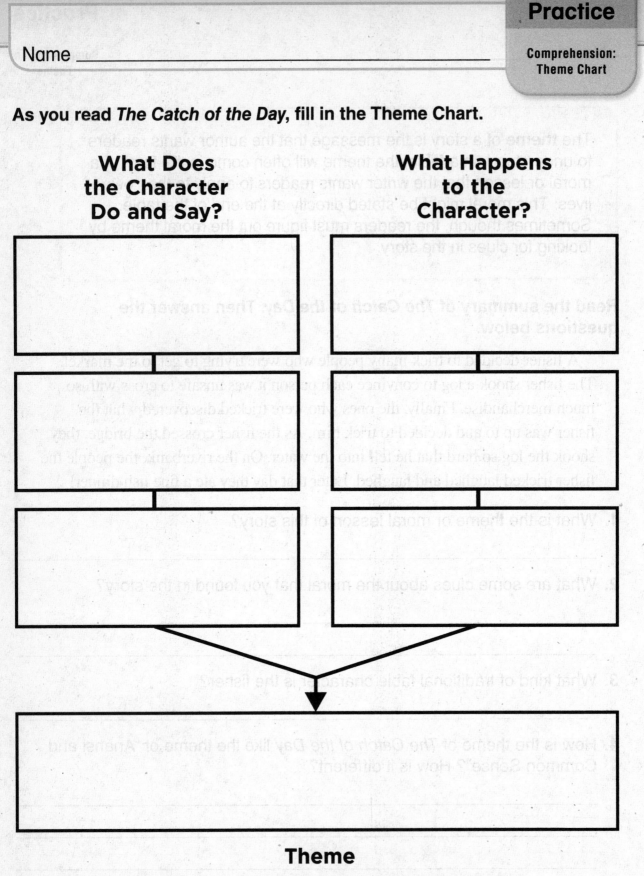

**What Does
the Character
Do and Say?**

**What Happens
to the
Character?**

Theme

How does the information you wrote in the Theme Chart help you
analyze the story structure of *The Catch of the Day*?

As I read, I will pay attention to rate.

	NARRATOR 1: Well, at least it isn't a raging river that Brer
11	Rabbit has to cross, just a creek. Though it is higher than
23	usual, and the rain is still coming down hard.
32	**BRER RABBIT:** (*to the audience*) Well, that wasn't too bad.
42	If getting my feet a little wet is the most **unfortunate** thing
54	that happens tonight, I'll be just fine. (*He shakes off the*
65	*wetness and looks around. Then, putting his hand to his ear,*
76	*he listens for a moment.*) Music! I do believe I hear a party
89	shaping up! (*He rubs his hands together eagerly.*) And that
99	means dancing, and dancing means food to feed the dancers,
109	and that means a fine time is had by all. (*He heads offstage*
122	*with a hop, skip, and a jump.*)
129	**NARRATOR 2:** And indeed, a fine time is had by all,
139	especially Brer Rabbit, who doesn't give another thought to
148	the weather. He tries every dance and every dish and finds
159	them all to his total satisfaction. 165

Comprehension Check

1. What does Brer Rabbit enjoy about parties? **Details**

2. How does Brer Rabbit feel about the weather? **Plot**

	Words Read	−	Number of Errors	=	Words Correct Score
First Read		−		=	
Second Read		−		=	

The **theme** of a story is the lesson that the writer wants to teach the reader. In some stories, especially fables or folktales, the theme is called the **moral**. Sometimes the writer clearly tells readers the theme. At other times, readers have to figure it out.

Read the passages below. Then compare the themes, or morals of the passages, by answering the questions.

A Chinese Fable

1.   A young man wanted to get a fox skin to please his new bride. He searched until he caught a fox by the tail. With great happiness at his success, he said to the fox, "My bride wants a fox coat. Can you give me your skin?"

    The fox recognized trouble and thought quickly about how to save himself. "I will be happy to do that, but I can't help you when you hold my tail so tightly. Please let go, and I'll immediately give you my skin." The man let go, and the fox ran away laughing.

A Greek Fable

2.   A wolf caught a young goat returning from the pasture. The goat knew that he couldn't escape, but he thought that he could fool the wolf. The goat said, "I know that you'll eat me, my friend, but I'd like just one favor from you. Would you play a tune so that I can dance once last time?" The wolf took out his pipes and played. Some dogs heard the music and became curious. They saw the wolf and began to chase him. The wolf knew that he'd been fooled. He said to the goat, "I got what I deserved; I'm a hunter, not a musician."

- What theme applies to the fox and the goat?

  _____

- These stories are alike, but they are from two different cultures. What does this difference tell you about the themes or the moral lessons in the stories?

  _____

Name _____

> **Similes** and **metaphors** are figures of speech that compare or associate two things. They use language to create striking or unexpected images for the reader. **Similes** use *like* or *as* in the comparison. **Metaphors** do not use *like* or *as*. Some similes have become common sayings, such as "busy as a bee".

Read the tale to answer the following questions.

One day Fox was strolling through the woods when Tiger crept up behind him as silently as a whisper. Then he pounced. Fox said, "Why are you trying to harm me? I am King of the Jungle."

Tiger was surprised. "You are as crazy as a monkey," he said. "You aren't King."

"Of course I am," Fox answered. "The other animals scatter like flies when they see me. Follow me." Fox went into the forest with Tiger behind him. When the deer saw Tiger behind Fox, they ran like the wind at the sight of them.

Then they came across monkeys. At the sight of Tiger behind Fox, the monkeys were statues, frozen in their trees. Then they fled.

Tiger said, "I'm as shocked as a child at a surprise party, but you are right. I'm sorry for bothering you, King." Tiger bowed to Fox, and Fox continued his walk.

1. What is one simile you can find in the tale? _____

_____

_____

2. How are the two things in the simile you chose related?

_____

3. What is the metaphor in the tale? _____

4. How is it different from a simile? _____

© Macmillan/McGraw-Hill

An **analogy** shows the relationship between two pairs of words.
In an analogy, the relationship between the two words in the first
pair is the same as the relationship between the two words in the
second pair. If the first pair is a pair of antonyms, so is the second
pair. If the first pair is a pair of synonyms, so is the second pair.

freeze	purchase	road	soar

**Choose a synonym or antonym from the box to complete each
analogy.**

1. Cash is to money as street is to _____

2. Car is to automobile as buy is to _____

3. Fall is to plummet as fly is to _____

4. Write is to erase as burn is to _____

**Create two antonym analogies and two synonym analogies of your
own.**

_____

_____

_____

_____

© Macmillan/McGraw-Hill

Name _____

A. Reading Strategy: Monitor and Adjust Comprehension

Make sure that you understand what you are reading. Comparing what you are reading to what you already know will help you. Choose a text that you are reading this week. Complete the chart for a difficult part of that text.

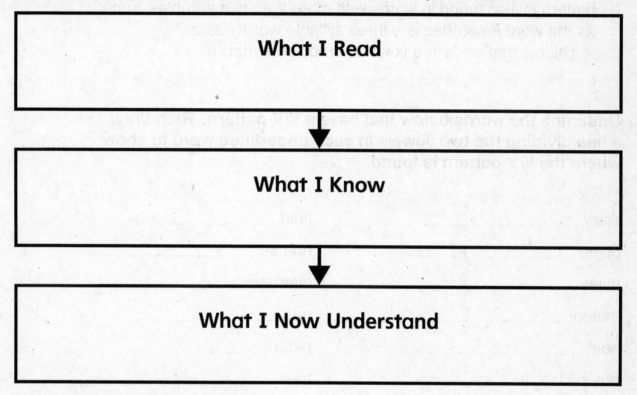

What I Read

What I Know

What I Now Understand

B. Independent Reading Log

Choose something you would like to read. After reading, complete the reading log. Be sure to tell the main idea or meaning of the text. Keep the details or events in the correct order. You may use the log to talk to others about what you read.

Genre _____

Title _____

Author _____

This Text Is About _____

_____

_____

Some words have a pattern with a syllable break between two vowels. This is called the **V/V pattern**. The word *fuel,* for example, has a syllable break between the vowel *u* and the vowel *e*. This pattern is also found in words with more than two syllables, such as the word ***idea***. Idea is a three syllable word: *i/de/a.*
A syllable that ends in a vowel is an **open syllable**.

Underline the words below that have a V/V pattern. Then draw a line dividing the two vowels in each underlined word to show where the V/V pattern is found.

diary _____

piano _____

minus _____

meteor _____

poet _____

riot _____

valley _____

casual _____

about _____

rodeo _____

closet _____

radio _____

fluid _____

hoarse _____

diameter _____

ruin _____

patriot _____

trial _____

diet _____

meander _____

cruel _____

fought _____

genuine _____

without _____

Name _____

A. Read each clue. Find the correct vocabulary word in the box, and write it on the line next to its clue.

accompany	consented	despair	delicacies
intentions	dismiss	descended	seek

Clues   **Vocabulary Words**

1. look for _____

2. went down _____

3. go with _____

4. hopelessness _____

5. agreed to _____

6. fine foods _____

7. goals _____

8. to send away _____

B. Write a vocabulary word to answer the questions and fill in the blanks below.

9. What is the opposite of did not allow? _____

10. The plane _____ before it landed.

11. What is the opposite of hope? _____

12. A lot of students like it when teachers _____ them from school early.

The **sequence** of events in a story is the order in which things happen. Determining the **chronological order** of events can help you summarize the action of a story by understanding how the events in the story relate to each other. Clue words such as *then, before, first, last, after, finally, when,* and *next* help readers follow a story's sequence.

Place the correct number for the chronological order of events in the left column next to the event described in the right column.

After Alexi spared the life of the Golden Mare, the horse became devoted to Alexi. Alexi became a huntsman for the Tsar. As his first order of business, Alexi captured the Firebird. Next, the Tsar asked Alexi to find Yelena the Fair so she could become his wife. Alexi persuaded Yelena to meet the Tsar. After Yelena discovered the Tsar's intention, she told the Tsar she would not get married without her grandmother's ring. The Golden Mare volunteered to fetch the ring from the lake. Yelena convinced the Tsar that she would turn a pot of water into a fountain of youth for him. The Tsar decided to test the water by having Alexi thrown in. Alexi survived and came out of the water with the ring. The Tsar was convinced that his youth would be restored, but he became an infant instead. Since he was too young to rule, Alexi became the Tsar and married Yelena. Alexi released the Firebird and the Golden Mare.

Order	Events from *The Golden Mare, the Firebird, and the Magic Ring*
	Alexi becomes a huntsman for the Tsar and captures the Firebird.
	Alexi spares the life of the Golden Mare, and the horse devotes her life to him.
	Yelena follows Alexi to meet the Tsar.
	Alexi is thrown into the cauldron of boiling water and survives.
	The Golden Mare volunteers to fetch Yelena's magic ring.

© Macmillan/McGraw-Hill

Name _____

Sequence Chart

As you read *The Golden Mare, the Firebird, and the Magic Ring*, fill in the Sequence Chart.

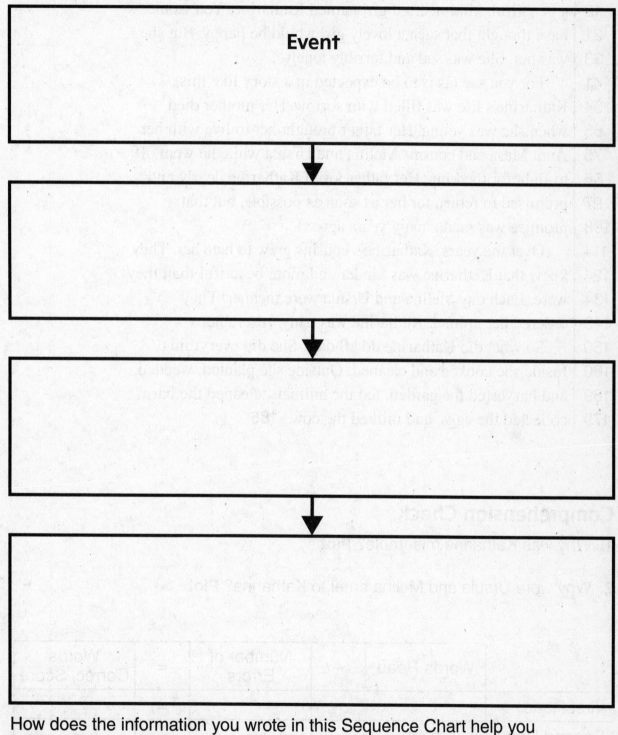

Event

How does the information you wrote in this Sequence Chart help you summarize *The Golden Mare, the Firebird, and the Magic Ring*?

The Golden Mare, the Firebird, and
the Magic Ring • **Grade 5/Unit 3**

103

Name _____

As I read, I will pay attention to expression and phrasing.

	Once upon a time, a really, really long time ago, there lived
12	a beautiful, kind-hearted girl named Katharine. You would
21	have thought that such a lovely girl would be happy. But she
33	was not. She was sad and terribly lonely.
41	For you see (as is to be expected in a story like this),
54	Katharine's life was filled with sorrow. Her mother died
63	when she was young. Her father brought her to live with her
75	Aunt Mara and cousins Melina and Ursula while he went off
86	to fight for the king. Her father loved Katharine dearly and
97	promised to return for her as soon as possible, but that
108	promise was made many years ago.
114	Over the years, Katharine's cousins grew to hate her. They
124	knew that Katharine was kinder and more beautiful than they
134	were. Each day Melina and Ursula were meaner. They
143	ordered her around. Katharine was truly miserable.
150	So what did Katharine do all day? She did everything!
160	Inside she cooked and cleaned. Outside she planted, weeded,
169	and harvested the garden, fed the animals, cleaned the barn,
179	collected the eggs, and milked the cow. 186

Comprehension Check

1. Why was Katharine miserable? **Plot**

2. Why were Ursula and Melina cruel to Katharine? **Plot**

	Words Read	–	Number of Errors	=	Words Correct Score
First Read		–		=	
Second Read		–		=	

Name _____

The point of view of a story relates to the person telling the story. A character in the story tells a story written in first-person point of view. A narrator who is not in the story tells a story written in **third-person point of view**. A story in **third-person omniscient point of view** tells the thoughts and feelings of all the characters. *Omniscient* means "seeing or knowing everything." A story in **third-person limited point of view** shares the thoughts and feelings of only one character.

Read the passages below. Then answer the questions.

1.   Billy was happy to teach Robbie to ride a horse. Billy was amazed that Robbie had never ridden before, but he thought that it would be rude to mention that. As they walked out to the barn, Robbie asked many questions. "Will the horse run fast? What if the horse won't move?" Billy shook his head and thought, "He might not know about horses, but maybe he knows about other things."

• Whose thoughts and feelings are given in the story? From which point of view is this story written? Explain your answer.

_____

_____

2.   Billy was happy to teach Robbie to ride a horse. Billy was amazed that Robbie had never ridden before, but he thought that it would be rude to mention that. Robbie was worried as they walked to the barn. When he looked at a horse, he saw was a huge, powerful animal. "How can I control something that big?" he wondered. Then he asked Billy, "Will the horse run fast? What if the horse won't move?" Robbie lived in the city and was used to riding a bike. Billy didn't understand why Robbie asked so many questions.

• Whose thoughts and feelings are told in the story? From which point of view is this story written? Explain your answer.

_____

_____

Name _____

A **Venn diagram** compares two things. Differences are written in the left and right circles. Similarities are written where the circles overlap.

A. Read the summary of *Cinderella*, and fill in the Venn diagram.

Cinderella

Cinderella is a household servant with an evil stepmother, evil stepsisters, and a fairy godmother. She loses a slipper at a ball, and the prince searches the kingdom for the woman to whom it belongs. Cinderella and the prince get married and live happily ever after.

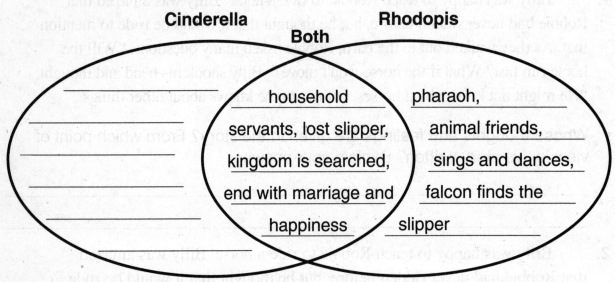

Cinderella   **Both**   **Rhodopis**

household servants, lost slipper, kingdom is searched, end with marriage and happiness

pharaoh, animal friends, sings and dances, falcon finds the slipper

B. Read the completed Venn diagram and write a summary of *Rhodopis*.

Rhodopis

_____

_____

_____

_____

_____

_____

© Macmillan/McGraw-Hill

Homophones are two or more words that sound the same but have different spellings and different meanings. You can use a print or electronic dictionary or glossary to check the different meanings, parts of speech, pronunciation, and syllabication of the homophones.

A. Circle the word that makes sense in each sentence.

1. Most fairy tales are stories that you have (herd / heard) before.

2. The hero often must race to complete a task in just one (hour / our).

3. In some stories, people try to (by / buy) happiness with jewels or gold.

4. My baseball team (one / won) the game.

B. Write a word from the box next to each word below to make pairs of homophones. Then write a sentence using one of the homophones in each pair.

pear	flower	course	hear

5. here _____

_____

6. coarse _____

_____

7. pair _____

_____

8. flour _____

_____

Name _____

A. Reading Strategy: Monitor and Adjust Comprehension

Make sure that you understand what you read. Forming scenes in your mind as you read will help you. Choose a text that you are reading this week, and complete the chart.

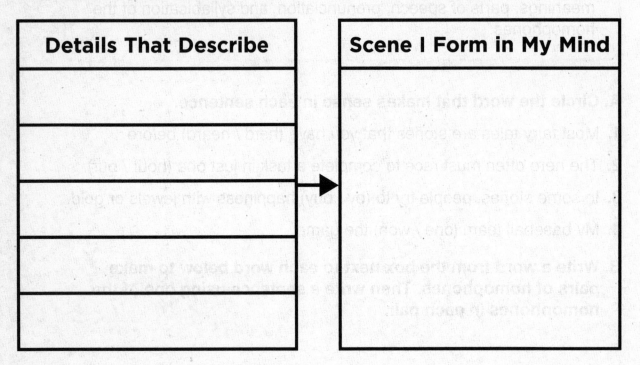

Details That Describe	Scene I Form in My Mind

B. Independent Reading Log

Choose something you would like to read. After reading, complete the reading log. Be sure to tell the main idea or meaning of the text. Keep the details or events in the correct order. You may use the log to talk to others about what you read.

Genre _____

Title _____

Author _____

This Text Is About _____

_____

_____

_____

© Macmillan/McGraw-Hill

Name _____

Every word has one or more syllables, and every syllable contains one vowel sound. Some vowel sounds are spelled with two letters. These letters form a **vowel team**. The two letters in each vowel team appear in the same syllable.

Often in vowel teams, the first vowel is long, and the second vowel is silent. When you read a syllable that contains a vowel team, try the long sound first. If the word does not sound right, then try another vowel sound.

Divide each word into syllables. Then underline the vowel team in each word. The first one has been done for you.

<u>lea</u>|ning

1. raining

2. grounded

3. Sunday

4. eighty

5. floated

6. bookshelf

7. meanest

8. soapbox

9. snowstorm

10. potpie

After you learn a new word, practice matching it with its definition and then using it in a sentence.

A. Read each word in Column 1. Match it with its definition in Column 2. Then write the letter of the correct definition on the line next to each vocabulary word.

Column 1

1. reveal ____

2. amusing ____

3. globe ____

4. generations ____

5. preserve ____

Column 2

a. the world

b. funny

c. to protect something so it does not change or disappear

d. to make known

e. groups of people born around the same time

B. Complete each sentence with the correct word.

6. People tell stories to _____ happy memories.

7. Dad told a story about Grandpa that was really _____.

8. Some tales have spread around the _____.

9. Lara would not _____ the end of the story.

10. Many _____ of people have enjoyed the story of "The Three Little Pigs."

Name _____

When you **compare** information, you tell how two or more things or ideas are alike. When you **contrast** information, you tell how they are different. Often, authors use signal words to show whether they are comparing or contrasting and to help readers make connections between ideas in a text.

Words for Comparing

like	too
both	also
and	similarly

Words for Contrasting

unlike	yet
but	
however	

Read the segment from the biography. Circle four signal words. Then answer the questions, using complete sentences.

Terrance had been at Grandma's house for two hours and was bored. Terrance lived in the city, but Grandma lived in the country. At home, Terrance could walk to the ball field by himself. But here, Grandma had to drive him. Unlike Terrance, Grandma didn't have a computer. Terrance was supposed to stay at Grandma's for a month; it would feel like a year.

Then Grandma showed Terrance a big plastic box full of old baseball cards. Terrance could see that he and Grandma were both big baseball fans. As they started to sort the cards, Grandma told Terrance stories about the players. Maybe summer at Grandma's would be fun after all!

1. What is one way that Terence and Grandma are different?

_____

2. What is one way that Terence and Grandma are the same?

_____

3. Compare and contrast the similarities and differences between a written biography and an oral story passed on by a storyteller.

_____

_____

_____

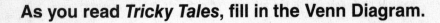

Name _____

As you read *Tricky Tales*, fill in the Venn Diagram.

Different

Alike

How does the information you wrote in this Venn Diagram help you
compare and contrast the stories in *Tricky Tales*?

Name _____

As I read, I will pay attention to phrasing.

"It's finally here!" I said to myself as I got off the school
13 bus that Friday afternoon. "And it's going to be great!"
23 I had been patient. I'd waited and waited for the big
34 family party. It was just one day away. From all over the city
47 and even as far away as Baltimore, my family was meeting
58 at our house for a cookout supper Saturday night. My older
69 sister, Mai, was excited, too. She had promised to decorate our
80 backyard and even string little lights all over the trees and
91 bushes. We'd start today, and then finish up tomorrow
100 morning before her big soccer game. I never missed Mai's
110 soccer games. She and her team were the city champions,
120 and their games were really fun to watch.
128   But now it was time to decorate the yard. 137

Comprehension Check

1. Why is the narrator excited? **Cause and Effect**

2. What is Mai's responsibility for the party? **Plot**

	Words Read	–	Number of Errors	=	Words Correct Score
First Read		–		=	
Second Read		–		=	

A **character** is a person or animal in a story. To understand a character, readers must pay attention to what the author directly states about the character; what the character does, says, or thinks; and how the character reacts to other characters. The **moral** of a story is its overall idea, or message about life.

A **trickster tale** is a folktale, often involving animals, in which one character tricks, or outsmarts, another character. A **fairy tale** is a folk story about real-life problems, usually with imaginary characters and magical events.

Read the trickster tale below. Then answer the questions that follow.

Coyote and the River

As Coyote walked along in the baking sun, he called out to the sky, "I would like a cloud to shade me." Sky sent a cloud to trail after Coyote, but Coyote was not satisfied and asked for rain. The small sprinkle sent by the cloud was not enough for Coyote, so he soon begged for more rain. The cloud sent a huge downpour.

Never happy, Coyote called out for a stream in which to wash his muddy feet. He demanded that the stream become deeper. It became a raging river that swept Coyote downstream and threw him on the riverbank.

And that is how the Columbia River was born.

1. How is Coyote similar to the Fisher in the play "Catch of the Day"?

_____

_____

2. Think about the fairy tale "The Little Mermaid" by Hans Christian Andersen. How are Coyote and the Little Mermaid alike? What is the moral, or lesson, of both tales?

_____

_____

_____

There are different ways to read a book or an article. **Skimming** is looking quickly over a passage to identify the important ideas. **Scanning** is searching for key words as you look over a text. Writing important information in the form of an outline is a good way to take notes. An **outline** is a summary that lists the most important ideas and details of a selection.

A. Read the passage below. Then answer the questions.

Recycle for the Future

Did you know that it takes more than 30 million trees to make a year's supply of newspapers? Recycling is an excellent way to preserve the environment and save some trees. Recycling one ton of paper saves 17 trees. When you recycle one aluminum can, you save enough electricity to run a TV for three hours. Recycling one glass bottle saves enough electricity to keep a light bulb lit for four hours. Taking a little time to recycle can help the environment in a big way!

1. Skim the passage. What is it mostly about? _____

_____

2. Scan the passage. What are some key words that you notice?

_____

B. Complete the outline so that it contains the same information as the passage.

Recycle for the Future

I. Recycling paper

    A. It takes _____ trees to make a year's supply of newspapers.

    B. Recycling _____ of paper saves _____ trees.

> **Homographs** are words that are spelled the same way but have different meanings and may have different pronunciations. You can use a dictionary to check the pronunciation of each word in a homograph pair.

A. Read each sentence. Circle the definition of the underlined word as it is used in the sentence.

1. Be careful not to <u>jam</u> your finger in the door.

   a. fruit spread   **b.** press or squeeze

2. The moral of the story is to be <u>kind</u> to others.

   a. friendly and helpful   **b.** the same type

3. We planted the carrots in a <u>row</u>.

   a. line   **b.** use oars to move a boat

4. <u>Close</u> the door so the dog does not run out.

   a. near   **b.** shut

5. I will <u>lead</u> my dog to the park on Sunday.

   a. a type of metal   **b.** show the way

B. Read the definitions for each homograph. Then write a sentence using one of the definitions.

6. palm   **a.** inside of a hand   **b.** kind of tree

   _____

7. rest   **a.** sleep   **b.** what is left

   _____

8. present   **a.** here; not gone   **b.** a gift

   _____

A. Reading Strategy: Monitor and Adjust Comprehension

Make sure that you understand what you are reading. Rereading parts of a text will help you. Choose a text that you are reading this week, and complete the activity.

1. Pause after you read a difficult part of the text. What is unclear about this part of the text? _____

   _____

   _____

   _____

2. Now reread that part of text. Reread more than once if needed. What does this part of the text mean? _____

   _____

   _____

   _____

B. Independent Reading Log

Choose something you would like to read. After reading, complete the reading log. Be sure to tell the main idea or meaning of the text. Keep the details or events in the correct order. You may use the log to talk to others about what you read.

Genre _____

Title _____

Author _____

This Text Is About _____

_____

_____

_____

_____

Many words end in a consonant and the letters *le.* In those words, the consonant and the letters *le* form the last syllable.

If the syllable before the last syllable ends in a vowel, it is an open syllable and has a long vowel sound. If the syllable before the last syllable ends with a consonant, it is a closed syllable and has a short vowel sound.

Read each consonant + *le* word below. Put a slash through the word to separate the syllables. Then look at the first syllable. If it is an open syllable, write *O* after the word. If it is a closed syllable, write *C* after the word.

1. stable _____

2. maple _____

3. candle _____

4. gentle _____

5. single _____

6. bubble _____

7. fable _____

8. apple _____

9. eagle _____

10. little _____

Name _____

Use the clues to complete the crossword.

consulted   detected   previous   proceeded
pursuit   recover   tasks   urgency

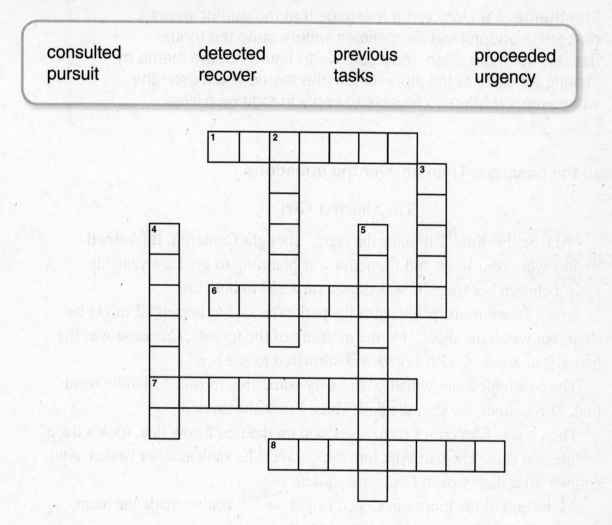

Across

1. the act of chasing someone
6. coming before in time or order
7. asked someone for information
8. noticed something

Down

2. become healthy again
3. jobs to do
4. the state of needing immediate attention
5. went on to do something

The **theme** of a story is the message that the author wants readers to understand. Sometimes writers state the theme directly, but more often, readers have to figure out the theme by looking for clues in the story. Often, the theme is a lesson the writer wants readers to be able to apply to their own lives.

Read the passage. Then answer the questions.

The Shortest Girl

"Maybe this time, I'll make the team," thought Cameron. Basketball tryouts were next week and Cameron was planning to go. Last year, she wasn't chosen because she was the shortest girl in her class.

Every Saturday she practiced at the park. She said to herself, "I might be short, but watch me shoot." On the morning of the tryouts, Cameron was the first girl to arrive. Coach Lopez was surprised to see her.

The coach blew her whistle. "Let's try some free throws." Maddie went first. Three times she shot the ball. Three times she missed.

Then it was Cameron's turn. She stood on the free throw line, took a deep breath, and shot. The ball sank into the basket. She sank another basket. And another after that! Coach Lopez was quiet.

At the end of the morning, Coach Lopez said, "You've made the team, Cameron!" Cameron wasn't surprised at all.

1. What can you tell about Cameron, based on what she does and says?

_____

_____

2. What message, or lesson, might the author want readers to learn?

_____

3. How is this story's theme similar to the theme of "The Party"?

_____

_____

© Macmillan/McGraw-Hill

As you read *Blancaflor*, fill in the Theme Chart.

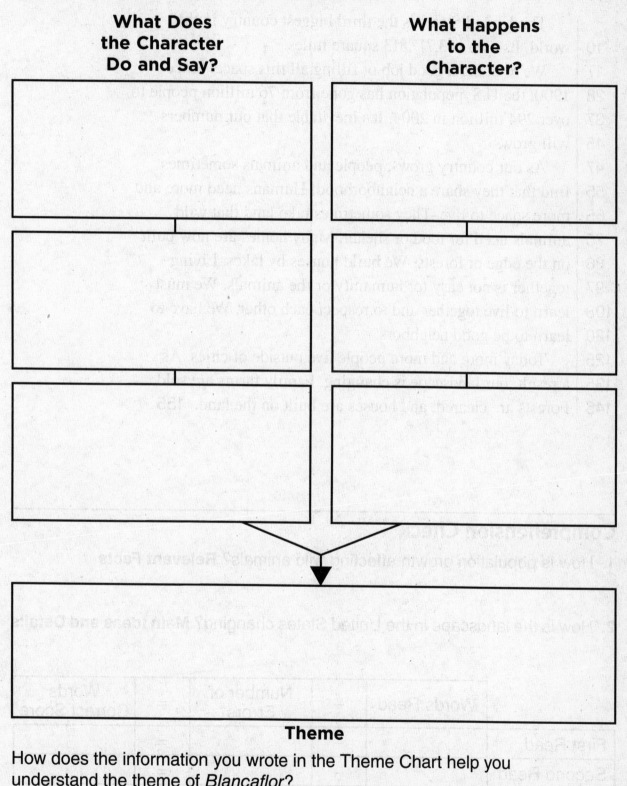

What Does the Character Do and Say?	What Happens to the Character?

Theme

How does the information you wrote in the Theme Chart help you understand the theme of *Blancaflor*?

As I read, I will pay attention to rate.

	The United States is the third biggest country in the
10	world. Its area is 3,717,813 square miles.
17	We're doing a good job of filling all this space. Since
28	1900, the U.S. population has gone from 76 million people to
37	over 294 million in 2004. It's inevitable that our numbers
45	will grow.
47	As our country grows, people and animals sometimes
55	find that they share a neighborhood! Humans need more and
65	more space to live. They sometimes take land that wild
75	animals need for food or shelter. Many homes are now built
86	on the edge of forests. We build houses by lakes. Living
97	together is not easy for humanity or the animals. We must
108	learn to live together and to respect each other. We have to
120	learn to be good neighbors.
125	Today more and more people live outside of cities. As
135	a result, our landscape is changing. Family farms are sold.
145	Forests are cleared, and houses are built on the land. 155

Comprehension Check

1. How is population growth affecting wild animals? **Relevant Facts**

2. How is the landscape in the United States changing? **Main Ideas and Details**

	Words Read	–	Number of Errors	=	Words Correct Score
First Read		–		=	
Second Read		–		=	

When you read **procedural text**, you are reading directions or steps that will help you complete a task, solve a problem, or perform a procedure. Usually, procedural texts are set up as lists with numbers or letters that show the steps to take. If a procedural text is in paragraph form, signal words such as *first, next,* and *finally* show the steps.

Read the passage below. Then fill in the chart. Paraphrase, or use different words, to tell each step.

Starting a School Club

In the past, students at our school have started clubs to enter science contests and put on plays. These are the steps to start a club. First, find other students who share your interest. You will need at least ten students to form a school club. Next, ask a teacher or other adult to be your advisor. They will help you meet the goals of your club. Then, register your club. Ask Ms. Jensen, the school secretary, for a club registration form. Fill out the form, have your parents and the advisor sign it, and return it to Ms. Jensen. Now you have officially started your club!

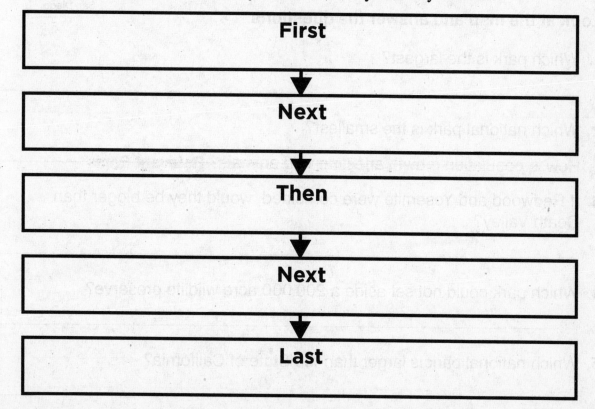

| First |
| Next |
| Then |
| Next |
| Last |

Name _____

A **table** helps to organize information for easy reference.

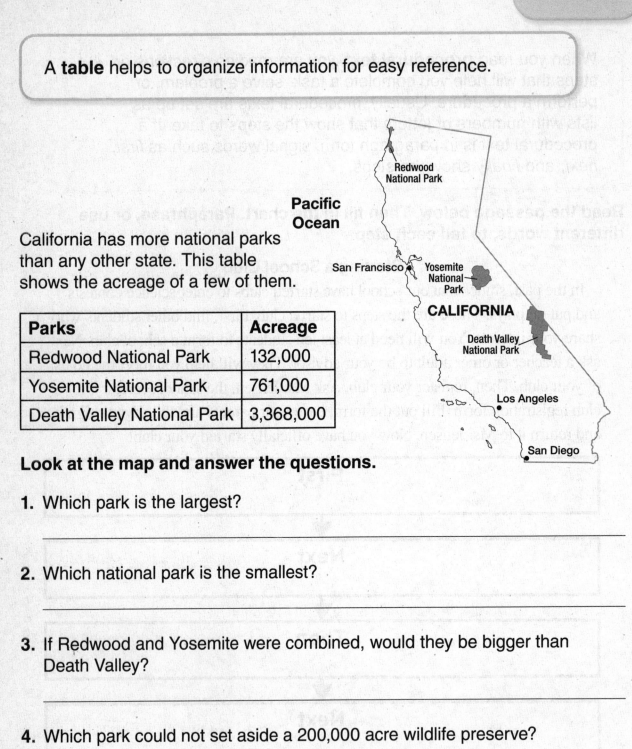

California has more national parks than any other state. This table shows the acreage of a few of them.

Parks	Acreage
Redwood National Park	132,000
Yosemite National Park	761,000
Death Valley National Park	3,368,000

Look at the map and answer the questions.

1. Which park is the largest?

_____

2. Which national park is the smallest?

_____

3. If Redwood and Yosemite were combined, would they be bigger than Death Valley?

_____

4. Which park could not set aside a 200,000 acre wildlife preserve?

_____

5. Which national park is larger than the State of California?

_____

Figurative language describes things by comparing them to other things that they are not literally or exactly like. Figurative language is often unexpected and tricky to figure out. To understand what an author means by figurative language, pay attention to the sentence or paragraph that contains it. Context clues can help you figure out the true meaning.

Maya *towered* over the smaller children in her kindergarten class.

The phrase *smaller children* is a clue that Maya is taller than the children. *Towered* means *stood tall, like a tower.*

Read each sentence. Circle the figurative language. Then explain the author's meaning in your own words. Use clues to help you understand the figurative language. The first example has been done for you.

Grandfather (was a rock); he helped all of his children through difficult times in their lives. Grandfather was strong and dependable.

1. LaTonya gleamed with pride as she won the spelling bee.

_____

2. When the swimmer finished the race, her lungs were on fire.

_____

3. Lara was a dragon if anyone tried to bully her little brother.

_____

4. It was difficult to see the trail after the blanket of night fell over the woods.

_____

5. Her eyes lit up when she found her lost kitten.

_____

Name _____

A. Reading Strategy: Monitor and Adjust Comprehension

Make sure that you understand what you read. Asking questions about a text will help you. Choose a text that you are reading this week, and complete this activity.

Pause after you read a difficult part of the text. Write a question about that part.

Question: _____

_____

Now reread that part of the text or read further, looking for clues that help you answer your question. Write the answer.

Answer: _____

_____

Repeat as needed as you continue reading.

B. Independent Reading Log

Choose something you would like to read. After reading, complete the reading log. Be sure to tell the main idea or meaning of the text. Keep the details or events in the correct order. You may use the log to talk to others about what you read.

Genre _____

Title _____

Author _____

This Text Is About _____

_____

_____

_____

_____

_____

Name _____

The **author's perspective** is his or her opinion or point of view about the topic. The perspective affects how a story is written because the author chooses words and a tone that show his or her opinions, feelings, and beliefs. Some authors base their themes on their opinions of real historical events.

Read each passage. Then answer the questions.

John raced up the trail, sending pebbles skidding behind him. When he reached his favorite hiding place, he fell to the ground out of breath. The river, full of late-summer rain, looked like a silver thread winding through his grandfather's farmland. They would be looking for him, but he was never coming down.

1. Explain the author's perspective on John's feelings.

_____

_____

2. What is the author's point of view about nature? How do you know?

_____

_____

His grandfather lifted him gently onto the horse. "The answer to that is in the code," he said. "The code name for America was 'Our Mother.' You fight for what you love. You fight for what is yours."

3. Explain how the author feels about the grandfather.

_____

_____

4. What do you think the author's point of view is on protecting the United States?

_____

_____

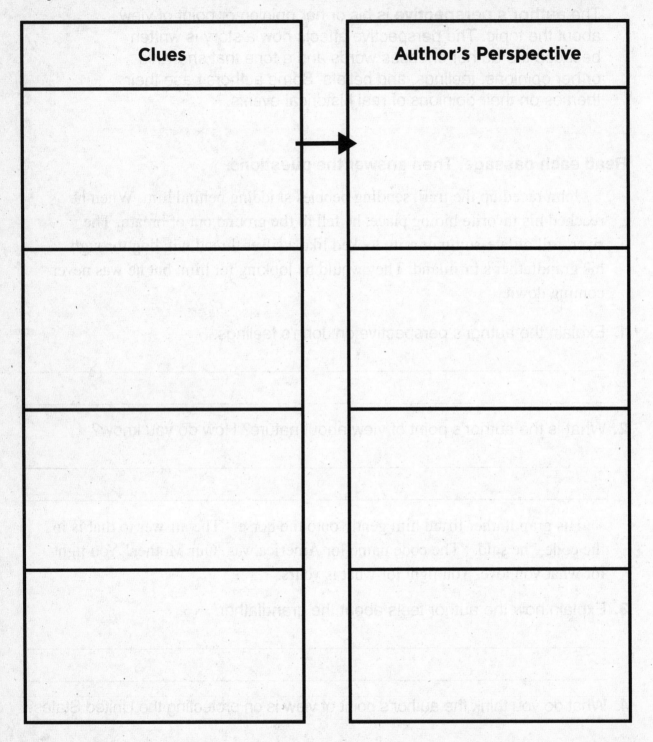

Name _____

As you read *The Unbreakable Code*, fill in the Author's Perspective Chart.

Clues	Author's Perspective

How does the information you wrote in the chart help you visualize
events in *The Unbreakable Code*?

© Macmillan/McGraw-Hill

As I read, I will pay attention to expression and phrasing.

8	During the American Revolution, a woman named Anna Smith Strong spied for the American patriots. She wanted to
18	help defeat the British, but she had to be very careful. If she
31	were caught, she would be sent to prison, or maybe even executed.
43	Anna Smith Strong thought of a simple way to pass
53	messages to the American patriots. She used her clothesline!
62	Everyone had to hang out laundry to dry in the 1700s. Who
73	would suspect that on her clothesline hung secret messages?
82	There were six coves near where Strong lived. The Americans
92	needed to know where a British ship was hiding. Strong used
103	her laundry to signal in which cove the ship was hiding. She
115	hung her black petticoat at one end of the line. Then she hung
128	up the correct number of creased white handkerchiefs to identify
138	the proper cove. Strong helped pass on important information—
147	and she was never caught. 152

Comprehension Check

1. How did Anna Smith Strong send secret messages to American patriots? **Main Idea and Details**

2. What would hang on Anna Smith Strong's clothesline if a British ship was hiding in the fourth cove? **Plot**

	Words Read	–	Number of Errors	=	Words Correct Score
First Read		–		=	
Second Read		–		=	

Comprehension:
Third-Person
Point of View

The story "The Unbreakable Code" is written from a **third-person point of view**. Third-person point of view means that a narrator who is not a character tells the story. When the narrator tells the thoughts and feelings of only one person, the point of view is **third-person limited point of view**. When the narrator tells the thoughts and feelings of all characters, the point of view is **third-person omniscient point of view**.

Read each passage. Then rewrite it, following the directions.

Grandfather looked at John, and a sad smile played across his lips. "Sometimes you must do what is difficult so that a greater good can be achieved." John felt his own heart crack at the thought of leaving.

1. Rewrite the passage from a third-person omniscient point of view.

_____

_____

_____

_____

Grandfather thought again about how they had spent the summer together and of how proud he was of John. He knew that he would miss his grandson, but he also knew that John belonged at school.

2. Rewrite the passage from a third-person limited point of view. You may choose either character as the source of the viewpoint.

_____

_____

_____

© Macmillan/McGraw-Hill

The Unbreakable Code
Grade 5/Unit 3

In poetry, **consonance** is the repetition of final consonant sounds in a series of words. **Symbolism** is the use of a concrete object or image to represent an abstract idea.

Read each cinquain below and then answer the questions.

Brother	1
Tell us about	2
Fellow brave and fearless	3
Navajo saved country and lives	4
And hope.	5

1. Which word shows consonance with *fearless* in line 3? _____

2. How could line 5 be rewritten to continue the consonance in line 4?

_____

Warning	1
Coding of words	2
In the puzzle of war	3
"Iron Fish" waiting underwater	4
Lives saved.	5

3. Which words in lines 3 and 4 show consonance? _____

4. The words "Iron Fish" probably symbolize which wartime vehicle?

_____

5. Why might using a symbol in a poem interest the reader more than simply

stating what the symbol represents? _____

_____

_____

You can often figure out what an unfamiliar word is by using **context clues**, which you can find by looking at other words in the sentence or in surrounding sentences.

Circle all the context clues that help you define the underlined word in each sentence.

1. During the drills, we said the same code over and over. We hoped that by <u>repeating</u> the code many times, it would be easy to remember.

2. Henry heard the wind always. The noise of the wind in the canyons especially was <u>ceaseless</u>. Its sound never stopped.

3. The <u>fierceness</u> of the Navajo Marines was well known. They were strong, brave, and powerful.

4. John felt <u>anxiety</u> about moving to Minnesota. He was nervous about living in a new place and worried about leaving.

5. Grandfather said that the code was a <u>triumph</u>. Each message was sent and received with success. Their goal had been reached!

6. Jen explained that only Navajos live on the <u>reservation</u>. The land is theirs to farm, protect, and enjoy.

7. Grandfather's face <u>wrinkled</u> as he laughed with his grandson. His cheeks scrunched up and lines appeared at the corners of his eyes.

8. When no rain fell, the leaves of Maria's favorite tree began to <u>wither</u>. They started to dry up and shrink.

© Macmillan/McGraw-Hill

A. Reading Strategy: Monitor and Adjust Comprehension

Make sure that you understand what you are reading. Using what you know, forming scenes in your mind, rereading, and asking questions will help you. Choose a text that you are reading this week, and answer these questions.

1. Which part of the text is unclear?

_____

_____

2. What is unclear about it?

_____

_____

3. Which strategy can you use to understand it?

_____

_____

4. How did using what you know, forming scenes in your mind, rereading, or asking questions help you?

_____

_____

B. Independent Reading Log

Choose something you would like to read. After reading, complete the reading log. Be sure to tell the main idea or meaning of the text. Keep the details or events in the correct order. You may use the log to talk to others about what you read.

Genre _____

Title _____

Author _____

This Text Is About _____

_____

_____

Name _____

Many words have unaccented final syllables. Some of these words end with the /əl/ sound, as you hear in the word **bottle**. Other words have a final /ən/ sound, as you hear in the word **sharpen**. The final /əl/ sound may be spelled as **-el**, **-le**, **-il**, or **-al**. The final /ən/ sound may be spelled as **-en**, **-in**, **-an**, **-on**, or **-ain**.

Circle the word in each pair that has a final unaccented syllable containing the /əl/ or /ən/ sound. Then write the letters that make the final sound in each word you circled.

1. human   moan   _____

2. winner   basin   _____

3. signal   prevail   _____

4. tell   angel   _____

5. nozzle   tale   _____

6. bacon   zone   _____

7. train   captain   _____

8. global   bale   _____

9. barrel   sell   _____

10. real   able   _____

11. listen   lessened   _____

12. practical   all   _____

13. slogan   lagoon   _____

14. will   pencil   _____

15. rain   mountain   _____

Name _____

abandon	treacherous	expedition	uninhabited
dismantled	labor	triumph	frigid

A. Write the vocabulary word that best completes each sentence.

1. Glaciers can be _____ because they have deep holes hidden under thin ice.

2. The scientist wanted to go on an _____ to the North Pole to learn more about the animals that live there.

3. Scientists _____ in the freezing weather to build a station.

4. The _____ water was hard for the boat to navigate through because of all the ice and snow.

5. People have been known to _____ over the tough environment at the North Pole.

6. They _____ the tents and packed the pieces onto the boat.

7. The early explorers had to _____ their shacks when they left Antarctica.

8. Until recently, Antarctica was _____ by humans.

B. Read each question. Then write the vocabulary word that best answers the question.

9. If you were on a special mission with a specific purpose, what would you be on? _____

10. What is another word for "be successful" or "win"? _____

11. If a building was not lived in for a very long time, what would it be?

_____

12. How would you describe a road with dangerous curves and no sidewalks?

_____

Read each of the following passages from *Spirit of Endurance*. In each passage, there is a problem and a related solution. Explain how Shackleton and his crew solved each problem.

The crew dismantled the dogloos and brought all the animals back on board because they were afraid that the ice would break under the dogs.

Problem: _____

_____

Solution: _____

_____

Luckily, the destruction of *Endurance* happened in slow motion. This gave the crew plenty of time to unload food and equipment. As the ship continued to break up, the pile of gear on the ice grew larger. Everything that could be taken off the ship was removed. The crew worked without a break. Their survival would depend on saving everything that might come in handy.

Problem: _____

_____

Solution: _____

_____

Their mountaineering equipment wasn't the best gear they could have wished for on a climb such as this one. They had an ax and 50 feet of rope. They studded the soles of their boots with nails for a better grip on the icy peaks. They rested for several days. Then, with food for three days and a small camping stove, they set out, crossing the first snowfield by moonlight.

Problem: _____

_____

Solution: _____

_____

© Macmillan/McGraw-Hill

Name _____

As you read *Spirit of Endurance*, fill in the Problem and Solution Map.

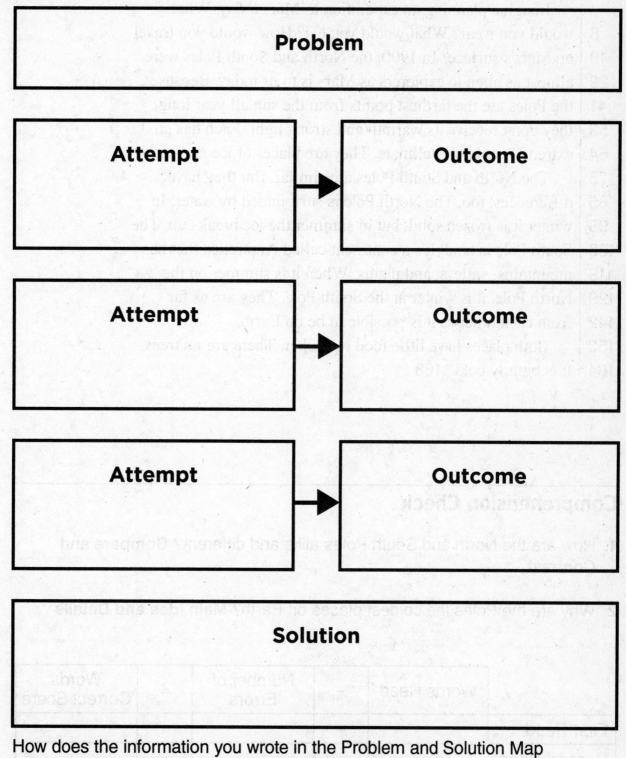

Problem

Attempt → **Outcome**

Attempt → **Outcome**

Attempt → **Outcome**

Solution

How does the information you wrote in the Problem and Solution Map
help you generate questions about *Spirit of Endurance*?

As I read, I will pay attention to rate.

	Imagine planning an expedition to Mars today. What
8	would you wear? What would you eat? How would you travel
19	on Mars's surface? In 1900, the North and South Poles were
29	almost as alien to explorers as Mars is to us today. Because
41	the Poles are the farthest points from the sun all year long,
53	they don't receive its warmth and strong light. Each has an
64	extremely cold, dry climate. They are places of ice and snow.
75	The North and South Poles are similar. But they have
85	differences, too. The North Pole is surrounded by water. In
95	winter it is frozen solid, but in summer the ice breaks up. The
108	South Pole is land. It's a continent called Antarctica that has
119	mountains, valleys, and plains. When it is summer on the
129	North Pole, it is winter at the South Pole. They are as far
142	from each other as it is possible to be on Earth.
153	Both places have little food or shelter. There are no trees.
164	It is bitterly cold. 168

Comprehension Check

1. How are the North and South Poles alike and different? **Compare and Contrast**

2. Why are the Poles the coldest places on Earth? **Main Idea and Details**

	Words Read	–	Number of Errors	=	Words Correct Score
First Read		–		=	
Second Read		–		=	

© Macmillan/McGraw-Hill

An **author's purpose** is the reason that an author writes something. Authors often write to inform, to entertain, to persuade, or to explain.

Read each passage. Then answer the questions.

1.   If you follow the arrow on a compass, where will you go? Some people think that they will go directly to the North Pole. This is not quite true. They will actually go to the North Magnetic Pole, which is close to the North Geographic Pole. The geographic pole is what most people think of as the North Pole. The magnetic pole is where Earth's magnetism is strongest. The magnetic pole moves around because it is made by melted rock under Earth's surface.

• What was the author's purpose for writing this passage? _____

• Which information presented by the author helped you draw a conclusion

  about the purpose? _____

• Do you think that the author achieved that purpose? _____

  _____

2.   I think our group should do a project on early explorers to the North Pole. These explorers led interesting lives. They faced great hardships to go on adventures. Many explorers did not survive. I think we should learn about them so that we can appreciate their courage.

• What was the author's purpose for writing this passage? _____

• Which information presented by the author helped you draw a conclusion

  about the purpose? _____

  _____

• Do you think that the author achieved that purpose? _____

  _____

  _____

A **primary source** is information that comes from the time being studied. **Journals** and **letters** are two types of primary sources. Journals provide daily records written by a person for his or her own use. Letters are a way for people to share information with others through writing.

Use the passage to answer the questions.

October 12

The group and I arrived safely in Antarctica today. The wildlife here is wonderful! I already have seen a colony of Adelie penguins and managed to make some sketches of them in my notebook.

The Adelie penguin

—has a white front and a black back.

—has a white ring around its eyes.

—is about 30 inches tall.

—weighs 11 pounds.

—eats fish. (Must remember to learn more about their diet tomorrow.)

1. What type of primary source is the passage above? How can you tell?

_____

_____

_____

2. In what ways does the primary source show that the author has witnessed the events described?

_____

_____

_____

3. Based on the passage, what is another primary source that you can expect to see with this one?

_____

_____

Name _____

A **base word** is a word that can stand alone. A **root word** is a word part that forms the core of a longer word. Base and root words can be changed by adding **affixes**. Affixes are word parts such as **prefixes** that are added to the beginning of a word or **suffixes** that are added to the end of a word. For example, the prefix *un-* means "not." The suffix *-able* means "able to." When these affixes are added to the root word *read*, they form the new word *unreadable*, meaning "not able to be read."

For each word, find the root or base word. Then rewrite the word, dividing it into its parts by drawing slashes. Underline the root or base word.

1. unbreakable _____

2. unkindness _____

3. independence _____

4. leadership _____

5. abandonment _____

6. international _____

7. worthless _____

8. autograph _____

9. preview _____

10. transportable _____

A. Reading Strategy: Make Inferences

Making inferences will help you understand what you read. You should support every inference with details from the text. Choose a text that you are reading this week, and answer these questions.

1. What question do you have that is not answered in the text?

   _____

   _____

2. What do you know that might help you answer the question?

   _____

   _____

3. What clues from the text might help you answer the question?

   _____

   _____

4. What inference can you make to answer the question?

   _____

   _____

B. Independent Reading Log

Choose something you would like to read. After reading, complete the reading log. Be sure to tell the main idea or meaning of the text. Keep the details or events in the correct order. You may use the log to talk to others about what you read.

Genre _____

Title _____

Author _____

This Text Is About _____

_____

_____

© Macmillan/McGraw-Hill

Name _____

A prefix is an affix added to the beginning of a root word. Adding a prefix always changes the meaning of the root word. Look at this list of prefixes and their meanings:

dis- means "not; opposite or lack of" *re-* means "again"
un- means "not; without"   *mis-* means "wrong, not"

Add one of the prefixes above to each of the words in the sentences below. Use context clues to help you decide which prefix to use.

1. Some people think my sister is _____usual because she wears sandals in the winter.

2. Gilda felt _____couraged about playing soccer after she missed a goal in her last game.

3. Tanya was looking forward to _____uniting with her extended family during her summer vacation.

4. Ben felt _____guided when his coach's advice didn't work out as planned.

5. Jackson _____understood the directions and turned right instead of left.

6. Tilly was _____aware that her little sister had picked up the other phone and was listening to her conversation.

7. I had to _____wrap the present after my baby sister tore the paper off.

8. When we returned to Argentina, we _____discovered the beautiful coastline.

9. "I'm sorry, but we'll be forced to _____connect your phone line if you won't pay the bill," said the representative.

10. "I didn't mean to _____lead you, sir; the elephant statue is not for sale," apologized the woman running the garage sale.

Name _____

A. Match each vocabulary word with its definition. Write the vocabulary word on the line provided.

mission	function	maze	environment
disasters	gravity	adjusted	zone

1. the air, water, soil, and all the other things surrounding a person, animal, or plant _____

2. special assignment or job _____

3. changed or rearranged _____

4. terrible and unexpected events _____

5. a confusing system of paths or passageways _____

6. to work properly _____

7. the force that attracts objects to Earth _____

8. an area set off from other areas _____

B. Answer each question.

9. Why is **gravity** important? _____

_____

10. How might a **maze** slow you down? _____

_____

_____

The **main idea** of a passage is what all of the **details** in a paragraph or passage have in common. It is what the text is mostly about. You can generate questions about what the details have in common in order to determine the main idea.

Read the two paragraphs below, and identify the details of the passage on the lines provided. Then use these details to determine the main idea.

Becoming an Astronaut

Astronauts must go through difficult training because just about everything is done differently in space. Astronauts must learn how to walk and work without gravity. They must practice wearing spacesuits. They must even learn how to eat and sleep while weightless.

Many different machines help the astronauts prepare for space travel. Some machines are simulators, or machines that re-create some of the conditions of outer space here on Earth. The 1/6 Gravity Chair simulates the moon's weaker gravity. On the moon, a person weighs one-sixth of what he or she weighs on Earth. In the Multi-Axis Trainer (MAT), astronauts experience what it is like to be in a tumbling spacecraft. The Five Degrees of Freedom (5DF) Chair simulates the challenges of floating weightlessly.

Details: _____

_____

_____

Main Idea: _____

_____

_____

As you read *Ultimate Field Trip* 5, fill in the Main Idea Chart.

Detail
Detail
Detail
Main Idea

Detail
Detail
Detail
Main Idea

Detail
Detail
Detail
Main Idea

How does the information you wrote in this Main Idea Chart help you generate questions about *Ultimate Field Trip 5*?

As I read, I will pay attention to accuracy.

	People on Earth have long looked at Mars with excitement
10	and fear. Mars is Earth's nearest neighbor and has an
20	environment similar to Earth's in many ways. The surface
29	of Mars is much like the surface of parts of Earth, dry and
42	hard. Temperatures on Mars range from -225° to 60°F
49	(-140° to 25°C). There are important differences, too.
55	The atmosphere of Mars is almost all carbon
63	dioxide and doesn't have enough oxygen to support humans.
72	On Mars, **gravity**, the force that pulls us toward the ground,
83	is not as strong as gravity on Earth.
91	However, of all the planets in the solar system, Mars
101	is the one that seems most possible for humans to visit and
113	even colonize. It is close to us, and it has a surface and
126	surface temperature most similar to that of Earth. 134

Comprehension Check

1. Why does Mars seem like the most likely planet for humans to visit? **Main Idea and Details**

2. What are some differences between Earth and Mars? **Compare and Contrast**

	Words Read	–	Number of Errors	=	Words Correct Score
First Read		–		=	
Second Read		–		=	

When you read **procedural text,** sometimes you will see maps, diagrams, illustrations, graphs, or tables. These graphic features help you understand the information as you read.

Read the procedural text. Then answer the questions.

Fire Rules

To be safe, follow these rules when you build a campfire.

1. Work under the supervision of an adult.
2. Tie back long hair and loose clothing.
3. Build your fire only in a fire pit area.
4. Use the wood stored near the fire pit. Use sticks and dry leaves as kindling for the fire.
5. Do not try to start a fire on a windy day.
6. Keep a pail of water nearby for emergencies.
7. Place kindling in the center of the fire pit.
   Make a teepee of sticks around the kindling.
   Build a box of larger sticks around the teepee.
   Place one or two split logs on the box.
   Light the fire carefully.
8. When cooking, use long-handled spoons.
9. When you are finished, pour water on the burning coals and smother them with dirt.
   Make sure that the fire is completely out before you leave the campsite.

Materials Needed for a Campfire
logs
dry leaves
sticks of varying sizes
matches
pail of water

1. What information does the table provide? _____

_____

2. With which two rules would an illustration of a pail of water be *most helpful?*

Why? _____

_____

© Macmillan/McGraw-Hill

Name _____

> **Symbolism** is the use of a concrete object or image to represent an abstract idea.
> The **moral** is the lesson a story teaches, which can then be used in real life. This moral might be stated directly at the end of the story. Sometimes, though, the readers must figure out the moral by looking for clues in the story.

Read the following story. Then answer the questions on the lines provided.

One day a huge lion caught a very small mouse in his claws. "Please let me go, and one day I will help you," said the mouse, pleading for his life.

But the lion just laughed. "How could such a small mouse ever help me, the big, strong king of the jungle?" But he let the mouse go, thinking it would be a good joke to eat the tiny fellow the *next* time they met.

The very next day, the big lion stepped out of his lair and into a hunter's net! He roared with anger and cried in fear. But he could not free himself.

The mouse heard the lion's cry and remembered his promise. He returned to the lion and started nibbling the rope that trapped him. Finally the lion was able to shake himself free.

The lion realized that the mouse had helped him after all. "Dear mouse, I was wrong to tease you for your size. You have saved my life!"

1. What does the mouse symbolize? _____

_____

2. What does the trapped lion symbolize? _____

_____

_____

3. Write the moral of the story in your own words. _____

_____

4. What object in the story symbolizes life's problems? _____

_____

Name _____

Practice

Vocabulary Strategy:
Context Clues:
Descriptions or
Explanations

If you are reading and come to an unfamiliar word, look at the other words in the sentence. These words might give you hints as to the meaning of the unfamiliar word. We call these hints **context clues**. For example, context clues might **explain** or **describe** an unfamiliar word.

Use context clues to help define the underlined words in the sentences. Circle the letter of the response that best completes each sentence.

1. At the U.S. Space Academy, we felt what it was like to be <u>weightless</u> and float through the air.

   If you are weightless, you are not affected by _____.

   a. air   **b.** gravity   **c.** space

2. Astronauts use <u>simulators</u> in order to feel like what it will be like in space.

   What are simulators? _____

   a. machines   **b.** portals   **c.** missions

3. Since space has no <u>atmosphere</u>, special suits need to be worn to supply astronauts with air and protect them from the sun.

   The special suits provide _____.

   a. sunlight and gravity   **b.** gas and bubbles   **c.** protection from the sun and air

4. The mission crew was asked to <u>deploy</u> the robot that was being stored to work on a broken satellite.

   In order to reach the satellite the robot had to be _____.

   a. sent out   **b.** destroyed   **c.** painted

5. Someday it might be possible to <u>colonize</u> the moon so people could live there.

   You cannot colonize a place without _____.

   a. sidewalks   **b.** people   **c.** bikes

© Macmillan/McGraw-Hill

Name _____

A. Reading Strategy: Make Inferences

Making inferences will help you understand what you read. You should support every inference with details from the text. Choose a text that you are reading this week, and complete this chart.

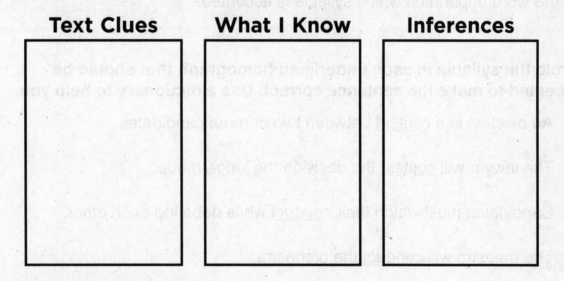

Text Clues	What I Know	Inferences

B. Independent Reading Log

Choose something you would like to read. After reading, complete the reading log. Be sure to tell the main idea or meaning of the text. Keep the details or events in the correct order. You may use the log to talk to others about what you read.

Genre _____

Title _____

Author _____

This Text Is About _____

_____

_____

_____

_____

Homographs are words that are spelled the same but have different meanings. Sometimes words that are homographs will be accented, or stressed, on different syllables. The part of speech and the meaning of the word depend on which syllable is accented.

Circle the syllable in each underlined homograph that should be accented to make the sentence correct. Use a dictionary to help you.

1. An election is a <u>contest</u> between two or more candidates.

2. The lawyer will <u>contest</u> the decision the judge made.

3. Candidates must watch their <u>conduct</u> while debating each other.

4. The maestro will <u>conduct</u> the orchestra.

5. The <u>conflict</u> was broadcast on television.

6. Luckily, her schedule did not <u>conflict</u> with ours.

7. Politics is a <u>subject</u> that many people feel strongly about.

8. The king did not <u>subject</u> his people to cruel punishments.

9. Every <u>minute</u> detail must be followed in the line of presidential succession.

10. A <u>minute</u> passed before I was called into the doctor's office.

11. He will probably <u>refuse</u> to run in the election.

12. Tim does not throw <u>refuse</u> in the recycling bin.

13. I am <u>content</u> to live in a democracy that offers so many freedoms.

14. The <u>content</u> of her speech was in the outline.

© Macmillan/McGraw-Hill

A. Write a sentence to answer each question. Make sure your sentence shows that you understand the meaning of the vocabulary word in the question.

1. What **supplies** might people need during the storm? _____

_____

_____

2. What is the most **violent** weather you have ever seen? _____

_____

_____

3. How can you get **involved** to help people after a bad storm? _____

_____

_____

4. What might be the **impact** if a tree fell on a house? _____

_____

_____

5. Which plants **survived** the storm? _____

_____

B. Now write a sentence using one of the vocabulary words.

6. _____

_____

_____

_____

_____

_____

_____

A **fact** is a statement that can be checked and proven true, such as *Marta is eleven years old*. An **opinion** is a statement of someone's beliefs or feelings and cannot be proven true, such as *Marta is the nicest girl in our class*. Some sentences include both facts and opinions. Opinions are not necessarily true or false, while a fact's truth can be verified.

A. Read the paragraph below. Underline the statements of fact. Circle the statements of opinion.

Last year, more than 15,000 people climbed Mount Shasta. At 14,162 feet, Mount Shasta is the tallest mountain in California. It is also the most beautiful.

Some of the climbers who reach the top of Mount Shasta have never climbed a mountain before. Others have climbed for many years. Seventeen different routes lead to the top of Mount Shasta. Mountain climbing is exciting and it is also very dangerous. People who climb with others have fewer accidents than people who climb alone.

B. Statements of fact can be checked and proven true. Write one statement of fact from the passage above. Then tell how you might check the statement of fact.

Fact: _____

Check: _____

Name _____

As you read *Heroes in Time of Need*, fill in the Fact and Opinion Chart.

Fact	Opinion

How does the information you wrote in the Fact and Opinion Chart help you monitor comprehension of *Heroes in Time of Need*?

As I read, I will pay attention to phrasing.

	The Mojave and Colorado deserts are two entirely
8	different ecosystems that exist side by side. Although they
17	are both arid, they look different, have different weather, and
27	are occupied by different living things.
33	These deserts are different because they are at two
42	different elevations, their height above sea level. The
50	Colorado Desert is below 3,000 feet in elevation. It has less
60	rainfall, fewer plants, and higher temperatures than the
68	Mojave Desert. The Mojave is over 3,000 feet in elevation.
77	It has more rainfall, and temperatures can dip below freezing.
87	So, Joshua Tree National Park contains two quite different
96	deserts. But the most remarkable thing about this park is
106	the area between the two deserts. This transition area is very
117	narrow, generally less than a mile wide. In this slim zone,
128	animals and plants from both sides of the park are abundant.
139	But the cholla (CHOY-uh) cactus rules the zone. Don't walk
148	too close to this "jumping" cactus or the spiny needles will
159	snag you. Ouch! 162

Comprehension Check

1. Compare and contrast the Mojave and Colorado deserts. **Compare and Contrast**

2. What is the transition area? **Relevant Facts**

	Words Read	−	Number of Errors	=	Words Correct Score
First Read		−		=	
Second Read		−		=	

© Macmillan/McGraw-Hill

Name _____

A **fact** is a statement that can be checked and proved to be true. An **opinion** is a statement that tells what someone believes. Opinions cannot be proved or disproved. It is important to verify facts by using fair and reliable sources of information.

Read the chart below. Then answer the questions.

Source	Strengths	Weaknesses
Television News	quickly reach many people; usually cite sources	may not have enough time to present the complete story
Newspapers	quickly reach many people; usually cite and check sources	may not have enough time to present the complete story
Magazines	reach many people; usually cite sources	may not have enough time to present the complete story
Web Sites	quickly reach many people; government and major media sites are usually reliable	can be hard to evaluate in terms of reliability; do not always cite sources
Encyclopedia Articles	very reliable; usually written by experts	are not updated as often as other media
Books	contain many facts and can cover subjects thoroughly	will not be available until well after an event has taken place

1. Which would be the *best* sources for information about a major disaster that happened in the last few days? _____

_____

2. If you wanted a short report on a disaster that happened several years ago, which source would be *best*? _____

3. Would you rather use a Web site or a printed news magazine as a source for information? Explain your choice. _____

_____

If you can identify the **parts of a book**, you can easily find the information that you need.

Read the chart below. Then write the correct part of a book to answer each question.

Front of a book	Back of a book
Title page: tells the book's title and author	**Index:** an alphabetical listing of names and topics and the page numbers that apply to each item
Chapter titles: tell the names of the chapters	**Glossary:** an alphabetical list of words and definitions
Table of contents: lists the chapter titles and the page number on which each chapter begins	**Endnotes:** notes that give additional information
	Bibliography: a list of writings that includes the date and place of publication

1. Where will you find notes that give additional information? _____

2. Where can you find the definitions of words? _____

3. Where are the book chapters listed? _____

4. Which two parts of a book are arranged in alphabetical order? _____

   _____

5. How could you learn whether a topic or person you are researching is

   mentioned in a book? _____

6. How could you find information about books or articles that an author used

   to write the book you are reading? _____

Some English words originally come from Greek or Latin words. Knowing the meaning of **Greek and Latin word roots** can help you figure out the meaning of unfamiliar words.

Greek Root	Meaning	Latin Root	Meaning
bio	life	aqua	water
pod	foot	port	carry
graph	write	man	hand

Circle the letter next to the correct meaning of each word. Use information from the chart to help you.

1. manual

a. done by a man, not a woman

b. done by hand

2. biopsy

a. a test for two eyes

b. a test of material from a living body

3. graphite

a. a mineral used for writing

b. a mineral that floats in water

4. aquatic

a. growing or living in water

b. moving quickly

5. podiatrist

a. a person who studies plants

b. a foot doctor

6. transport

a. to carry from one place to another

b. to play a game in different places

A. Reading Strategy: Make Inferences

Making inferences will help you understand what you read. You should support every inference with details from the text. Choose a text that you are reading this week, and complete this chart.

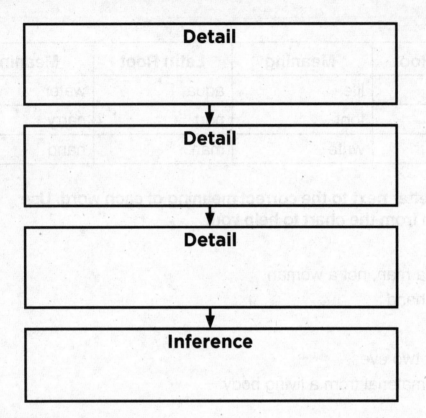

B. Independent Reading Log

Choose something you would like to read. After reading, complete the reading log. Be sure to tell the main idea or meaning of the text. Keep the details or events in the correct order. You may use the log to talk to others about what you read.

Genre _____

Title _____

Author _____

This Text Is About _____

_____

Name _____

The sounds you hear in the final syllable of the words *culture* and *measure* can be spelled in different ways, including **-ture** and **-sure**. Listen to the final syllables in the words *measure* (**/zhər/** sound) and *culture* (**/chər/** sound).

A. Choose the word in each pair that has a final syllable that sounds like /zhər/, as in *measure*. Then write the word on the line.

1. vulture / closure   _____

2. pleasure / rancher   _____

3. exposure / fracture   _____

4. mixture / treasure   _____

5. enclosure / picture   _____

6. leisure / fixture   _____

B. Choose the word in each pair that has a final syllable that sounds like /chər/, as in *culture*. Then write the word on the line.

7. legislature / leisure   _____

8. future / composure   _____

9. fixture / pleasure   _____

10. assure / nature   _____

11. mixture / erasure   _____

12. pasture / ledger   _____

13. creature / enclosure   _____

14. pressure / gesture   _____

15. exposure / nurture   _____

Name _____

A. Label each sentence *True* if the boldface vocabulary word is used correctly. If a sentence is *False*, explain why on the line below.

1. A **defective** toy is in good working order. _____

   _____

2. If positions are **reversed** during a class debate, your team begins arguing for the opposite opinion. _____

   _____

3. A **meteor** comes from deep inside Earth. _____

   _____

4. A **robot** is a living thing. _____

   _____

5. If you see a tree branch that is **dangling**, it is lying on the ground. _____

   _____

6. My sister played with a spinning top that **rotated** in circles. _____

   _____

7. The tired runner **staggered** to the finish line, looking as if he might fall down.

   _____

8. You might use the **tokens** from a board game to buy lunch. _____

   _____

B. Write two sentences that each includes one vocabulary word.

9. _____

   _____

10. _____

    _____

© Macmillan/McGraw-Hill

Name _____

As you read, you can **draw conclusions** by connecting information the author provides with what you know from your own related knowledge. This helps you analyze and better understand a story and its characters.

Read the two paragraphs below, then answer the questions. Describe the clues that helped you draw a conclusion.

It was almost noon. Maria had been watching the clock for the last half hour. Wouldn't Mrs. Jones ever stop talking? Maria thought again of the green apple in her lunchbox. She could almost taste it. Then her stomach began to growl.

What conclusion can you draw about Maria? _____

_____

Story clues: _____

_____

Experience clues: _____

_____

Evan picked at his cereal. He knew he should have studied harder last night, but the dates all ran together in his head. Why did he have to learn American history anyway? For the third time, his mother told him to hurry. He put on his coat. He felt a sudden wave of dread.

What conclusion can you draw about Evan? _____

_____

Story clues: _____

_____

Experience clues: _____

_____

Name _____

As you read *Zathura*, fill in the Conclusions Diagrams.

Evidence   Conclusion

Evidence   Conclusion

How does the information you wrote in the Conclusions Diagrams help
you monitor comprehension of *Zathura*?

As I read, I will pay attention to expression and phrasing.

	Robomation was Gregory and Anthony's favorite
6	magazine. It had articles about space exploration, science
14	experiments kids could do at home, and stories about
23	traveling to other planets. Plus, winners of the contests got
33	out-of-this-world prizes. Or so Gregory heard. He had yet to
43	win a single contest despite many, many tries.
51	"Gregory! Anthony!" That was Gregory's mom calling
58	them from the kitchen. From her tone, Gregory could tell
68	there was something she wanted him to do, and he dreaded it.
80	"Yes, Mom," he answered right away. "What is it?"
89	"Why don't you go outside?" she called out. "It's such a
100	beautiful day. Go get some fresh air and exercise. A bunch of
112	kids are shooting baskets across the street."
119	Gregory knew his mother was talking about Jordan Veras
128	and the "cool" gang. Gregory didn't fit in with their group,
139	though he had tried often. Maybe, if he were someone else. . . .
150	"Okay, Mom," Gregory sighed. He knew his mom was
159	right about the exercise. 163

Comprehension Check

1. Why was *Robomation* Gregory and Anthony's favorite magazine? **Details**

2. Why isn't Gregory excited about going outside? **Plot**

	Words Read	–	Number of Errors	=	Words Correct Score
First Read		–		=	
Second Read		–		=	

Text features such as **illustrations** and **captions** add factual
and quantitative information to reading material. An illustration
may appear as a photograph, a drawing, or a painting. A caption
uses words to label or explain the illustration. Text features also
include **headings**. A heading appears in large type and provides
a preview of the text that follows. Text features such as boldface,
italic, and highlighted type draw attention to important words and
new vocabulary. In online articles, text features include **toolbars**
and **links**. Toolbars help readers move around within a Web site,
and links allow readers to jump to other Web sites. By examining
text features, readers can gain an overview of the text and locate
specific information about the topic.

**Use the passage on pages 478–481 in your book to answer these
questions.**

1. What can you learn about the topic of the selection by examining the text

   features? _____

   _____

2. Which link on page 478 would you use to find the name and location of the

   world's largest telescope? _____

3. Which words on pages 478–479 appear in boldface and highlighted type?

   _____ Why do these words appear

   in boldface and highlighted type? _____

   _____

4. What does the illustration on page 479 show? _____

   _____

5. Whose portrait appears on page 479? _____

   Why is this person's portrait included in the selection? _____

   _____

Name _____

A **toolbar** is a strip of symbols that allows you to do specific actions with a Web page or document. A **link** is an electronic connection on a Web site that provides direct access to other information.

Use the Web site page to answer the questions.

1. What buttons can you find on the toolbar? _____

_____

2. How can links help you get information? _____

_____

3. On this Web site, how would you get information about Galileo's life?

_____

4. What would you select to learn about current astronomers?

_____

An **analogy** is a comparison of two pairs of words. **Synonyms**, or words with the same meaning, can be used in analogies. The two words in the first pair match in the same way that the two words in the second pair match.

Read this example: Big is to large as thin is to _____slim_____.

The words **big** and **large** are synonyms, and the words **thin** and **slim** are synonyms.

A. Complete each analogy by writing a synonym for the first word in the second pair of words.

1. Take is to grab as break is to _____.

2. Freedom is to liberty as talk is to _____.

3. Find is to discover as work is to _____.

4. Try is to attempt as shiver is to _____.

5. Car is to automobile as column is to _____.

6. Location is to place as choose is to _____.

B. Create two synonym analogies of your own.

_____

_____

_____

_____

Name _____

A. Reading Strategy: Make Inferences

Making inferences will help you understand what you read. You should support every inference with details from the text. Choose a text that you are reading this week, and complete this chart.

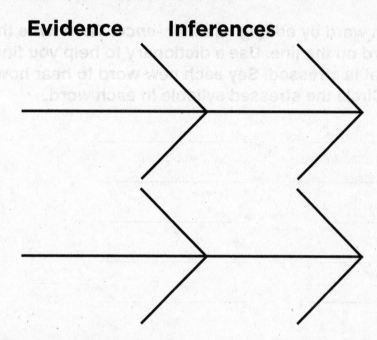

Evidence   **Inferences**

B. Independent Reading Log

Choose something you would like to read. After reading, complete the reading log. Be sure to tell the main idea or meaning of the text. Keep the details or events in the correct order. You may use the log to talk to others about what you read.

Genre _____

Title _____

Author _____

This Text Is About _____

_____

_____

_____

Name _____

The suffixes *-ance* and *-ence* mean "the state or quality of." They are suffixes with unstressed vowels.

Complete each word by adding *-ance* or *-ence*. Then write the completed word on the line. Use a dictionary to help you find the syllable that is stressed. Say each new word to hear how it is pronounced. Circle the stressed syllable in each word.

1. ambul_____   _____

2. resid_____   _____

3. bal_____   _____

4. subst_____   _____

5. import_____   _____

6. assist_____   _____

7. abs_____   _____

8. persist_____   _____

9. attend_____   _____

10. disturb_____   _____

11. independ_____   _____

12. perform_____   _____

13. refer_____   _____

14. eleg_____   _____

15. emerg_____   _____

Name _____

A. Match the vocabulary word with its definition. Then write the letter of the correct word on the line.

1. ease _____
2. scenery _____
3. bundle _____
4. fused _____
5. guaranteed _____
6. supervise _____
7. frustrated _____
8. coordination _____

a. joined together
b. disappointed or kept from doing something
c. working well together
d. move carefully or slowly
e. landscape
f. group of things held together
g. assured
h. watch and direct

B. Fill in the paragraph using the eight vocabulary words from section A.

My uncle _____ that we would enjoy the

_____ of the mountains and lake. But the trip did not start out

great. We tried to _____ the tent out of the stuffed car, but it

wouldn't budge. Next, my older brother became _____ when

he noticed the _____ of hamburgers was _____

together. Unfortunately, we did not bring any other food for dinner. We relied

on the _____ of all three of us to get the hamburgers

separated. While my uncle cooked, he wanted to _____ me as

I unpacked the rest of the car. I was about to ask to go home when I saw two

baby deer playing with each other. I guess being in nature is worth a frozen

dinner and overstuffed car.

Describing the **characters** (people and animals in the story) and the **setting** (where and when the story takes place) and how they relate to each other and the plot can help you better understand a story.

Answer each question below. Then explain your answers.

1. It takes Uncle Curtis three tries to find the exit to Mount Tamalpais. When Uncle Curtis finally makes it to the park, he is given a map of the campgrounds. He "didn't even glance at it but threw it into the backseat." Do you think he made a wise decision when he chose to ignore the map?

    _____

    _____

    _____

2. Teddy and Bobby wear clothes appropriate for a San Francisco summer—sweatshirts and corduroys. The weather forecast for Mount Tamalpais is hot and humid. Teddy and Bobby decide to pack only sweatshirts and corduroys to take to the camp. What do you think of their clothing decision?

    _____

    _____

    _____

3. Teddy and Bobby find that the hot dogs and hamburgers, which Teddy had packed in dry ice, are frozen solid. But Uncle Curtis tries to grill the frozen food before it has thawed. Do you think that Teddy's method of packing the meat was successful?

    _____

    _____

    _____

    _____

© Macmillan/McGraw-Hill

Name _____

As you read *Skunk Scout*, fill in the Character and Setting Chart.
Include information about how the characters relate to each other.

Character	Setting

How does the information you wrote in this Character and Setting Chart
help you monitor comprehension of *Skunk Scout*?

Name _____

As I read, I will pay attention to expression.

9	Can you guess what main force created the Grand Canyon? It was the mighty Colorado River.
16	The Colorado is a huge, powerful river. In the spring,
26	melted snow fills the river, and it becomes swift and wild.
37	The river picks up rocks, huge boulders, sand, and pebbles
47	and carries them along. Over millions of years, this gritty
57	river water carved into layer after layer of rock. It carved the
69	deepest canyon of all, the Grand Canyon.
76	One reason the river could carve the rock is that the rock
88	was soft. Soft for rock, that is! Back in time, before there was
101	a Grand Canyon, oceans covered the land.
108	Over millions of years, broken seashells, sand, mud, and
117	clay fell to the bottom of the sea. These small bits of matter
130	that settle on the sea bottom are called sediment. Over
140	millions of years, the sediment turned into rock, called
149	sedimentary rock. And this rock was soft enough for the river
160	to be able to carve a deeper and deeper path through it.
172	But the Colorado River was not the only force to form the
184	Grand Canyon. 186

Comprehension Check

1. How did the Colorado River help form the Grand Canyon? **Main Idea and Details**

2. What is sedimentary rock? **Relevant Facts and Details**

	Words Read	–	Number of Errors	=	Words Correct Score
First Read		–		=	
Second Read		–		=	

© Macmillan/McGraw-Hill

Name _____

A **primary source** is a text that contains information provided by a person who experienced an event. Journals and letters are two types of primary sources. Interviews with eyewitnesses are also primary sources. Sometimes authors write about events that they did not experience. These texts are called **secondary sources**. Secondary sources are based on primary sources. They often appear as news or magazine articles that contain information gathered by reporters. Books are another kind of secondary source when they are written by someone who did not witness an event.

Read each passage. Then answer the questions.

1.   **February 3**

I can't believe what just happened! I was out walking with Caitlin, and a skunk just crossed our path! We were so amazed that we would see this kind of wildlife in the middle of the city! I'm glad that we had our camera with us, so that we could take a quick photograph of the surprise!

- Is this a primary or secondary source? How do you know?

_____

_____

2.   **Wildlife Invades City**

City folks are getting new neighbors of the four-footed type. At least that was the experience of twin sisters Caitlin and Claire Magetti last Sunday. The twins were walking to a friend's home when a skunk crossed in front of them. "It was just there, clear as day. It didn't spray us or anything. It just turned around and walked off," said Claire. The sisters took this photograph of their new neighbor.

- Is this a primary or secondary source? How do you know?

_____

_____

Name _____

An **interview** is a conversation in which one person asks another person questions and records the answers.

Read the following interview. Then answer the questions that follow.

Reporter: Can you please state your full name and occupation?

Maria Chavez: Maria Chavez, fifth-grade teacher.

Reporter: Ms. Chavez, how is it that you became a teacher?

Chavez: I have always loved kids. As a young girl growing up in Mexico, I always took care of the children in the neighborhood. I loved to babysit for my cousins, and I enjoyed helping them with their schoolwork. I liked helping them learn! So, when I graduated from college, I thought teaching would be the best way to make a living and do what I am good at. I chose fifth grade because I think this is the most exciting year of elementary school.

Reporter: Do you have a favorite subject to teach?

Chavez: I like them all. I enjoy teaching English because we get to read so many wonderful stories, but when it's time to start math or science, I roll up my sleeves for that, too! I just think it's all so exciting.

1. Who is the reporter interviewing?

_____

2. Who is this person?

_____

_____

3. What led her to her current profession?

_____

_____

4. Where did Ms. Chavez grow up?

_____

Words with more than one meaning are **multiple-meaning words**. You can use **context clues**, or other words in the sentence, to help you figure out the meaning. Sometimes you must use a **dictionary** to learn the different meanings of the word.

A. Read each sentence. Then circle the letter next to the correct meaning of each underlined word.

1. My first camping trip <u>might</u> have been a disaster, but it turned out great.

   a. physical strength   **b.** expressing possibility or doubt

2. We had to change a flat tire on the way to the campground, but the <u>spare</u> tire worked fine.

   a. extra   **b.** hold back or avoid

3. After that, we set up our tent near some trees and <u>brush</u>.

   a. object with bristles on a handle   **b.** heavy growth of bushes

4. <u>Cavities</u> in the rocks near the river were the perfect place to store our towels while we swam in the lake.

   a. hollow places   **b.** decayed spots on teeth

5. He still had some <u>change</u> in his pocket.

   a. to become different   **b.** coins

6. As the day came to a <u>close</u>, I was happy to be camping.

   a. end   **b.** shut

B. Use a dictionary to find two meanings of each multiple-meaning word listed below.

7. jam   **a.** _____

          b. _____

8. coat   **a.** _____

          b. _____

A. Reading Strategy: Make Inferences

Making inferences will help you understand what you read. You should support every inference with details from the text. Choose a text that you are reading this week, and complete the activity.

Before Reading Note the kinds of inferences that you might make while reading the text.

I will read	I might make inferences about
Fiction/Drama	characters' actions, events, the author's message
Poetry	the speaker's meaning, the author's message
Biography/Autobiography	the subject's actions, events, the author's message
Informational Text	causes and effects, problems and solutions
Persuasive Text	the author's message, ideas used to support the author's message

During Reading Use ideas from the chart and clues from the text to make inferences.

After Reading Explain how you used an idea from the chart and clues from the text to help you make an inference.

B. Independent Reading Log

Choose something you would like to read. After reading, complete the reading log. Be sure to tell the main idea or meaning of the text. Keep the details or events in the correct order. You may use the log to talk to others about what you read.

Genre _____

Title _____

Author _____

This Text Is About _____

_____

_____

© Macmillan/McGraw-Hill

A **suffix** is a word part added to the end of a root word to change its meaning. Adding a suffix sometimes changes the spelling of a root word.

happy + **-ly** = happily   forget + **-able** = forgettable
argue + **-ment** = argument

Combine the word parts to write a word with a suffix. Remember to make any necessary spelling changes. Then use each word in a sentence.

1. close -ly _____

2. observe -tion _____

_____

3. microscope -ic _____

_____

4. knowledge -able _____

_____

5. concentrate -ion _____

_____

6. care -ful -ly _____

_____

7. happy -ness _____

_____

8. enjoy -able _____

9. strategy -ic _____

_____

10. beauty -ful _____

_____

Complete each sentence by choosing the best word from the box.

eldest	depicts	detested	ignored
refuge	projects	obvious	obedience

1. Sir Francis Drake, the first English explorer to reach California, was the _____ of 12 sons.

2. Drake went to sea as a young man, and it was soon _____ that he would be a great sailor.

3. Drake and the other sailors spent long days doing _____ on their ship.

4. Sailing across the sea was very dangerous, but sailors _____ gloomy warnings.

5. When they were caught in storms, sailors found _____ on quiet islands.

6. A painting _____ Drake meeting with Native Americans in California.

7. Some explorers from Spain _____ Drake and his crew, claiming that the English stole money from them.

8. Drake is remembered for his bravery and for his _____ to Queen Elizabeth I.

Name _____

As you read a story, look for **cause-and-effect** relationships. A **cause** is an event or action that makes something happen. An **effect** is the result of the cause. For example, if settlers in an area use up one source of food, they will look for another source. The first event (using up one source of food) is the cause, and the second event (looking for a new source) is the effect. Understanding cause and effect helps you understand why events in a text happen, what will probably happen next, and how all the events in a text are related.

Writers use signal words and phrases such as *because*, *so*, *as a result*, and *then* to show cause-and-effect relationships.

Read the following article. Circle the signal words that show cause-and-effect relationships. Then, on the lines below, write four pairs of causes and effects.

About 13,000 years ago, hunters from the north came to the area that is now the western United States so they could hunt the large animals that lived there. After a while, the animals died out and then the people could not find enough food to eat. Because they were hungry, the people started to raise crops. As a result, they started living in villages.

1. cause _____

effect _____

2. cause _____

effect _____

3. cause _____

effect _____

4. cause _____

effect _____

Name _____

As you read *Valley of the Moon: The Diary of María Rosalia de Milagros*, fill in the Cause and Effect Chart.

Cause	➡	Effect
	➡	
	➡	
	➡	
	➡	
	➡	

How does the information you wrote in this Cause and Effect Chart help you be more aware of cause-and-effect relationships as you read *Valley of the Moon: The Diary of María Rosalia de Milagros*?

As I read, I will pay attention to my expression.

	I handed in my Jupiter report today, but I don't remember
11	anything about the planet. That's because as soon as I got
22	home, excitement ruled. I could hear the noise about half a
33	mile away. When I got to the farm, there was bedlam!
44	"Well, if you didn't plant it, then how did it get here?"
56	I heard my mother yelling. My father said he didn't know how
68	the peculiar plant got there but that it had to be gotten rid of
82	right away. He didn't want our crop to be spoiled by some
94	mystery fruit.
96	"Hey, what's going on?" I asked over all the commotion.
106	"This!" shouted my mother as she pointed to a strange tree
117	in the middle of the orchard.
123	At first glance, when I looked at the tree, it looked like all
136	the other trees. But then I noticed the extraordinary fruit. Each
147	piece was round and yellow and had a big red spot on it. There
161	was just one spot and each piece of fruit was the same. 173

Comprehension Check

1. What is the problem? **Problem and Solution**

2. Why does the father plan to get rid of the tree? **Details**

	Words Read	–	Number of Errors	=	Words Correct Score
First Read		–		=	
Second Read		–		=	

© Macmillan/McGraw-Hill

When you read on your own, you can take steps to make sure that you understand what you are reading. For example, you can **paraphrase** sections of text. When you paraphrase, you retell something in your own words. Also, you can **summarize** sections of text or a text as a whole. When you summarize nonfiction text, you retell main ideas and the most important details. When you summarize a story, you tell about the characters, setting, and plot. A summary is much shorter than the original work. As you summarize and paraphrase, keep the meaning of the text clear, and keep ideas from the text in an order that makes sense.

Conduct research to find a historic diary or a work of historical fiction. Read the selection. Then write the title of the selection, and complete the chart. In the first column of boxes, record challenging sections of the text. In the second column of boxes, paraphrase each section. In the box at the bottom, summarize the text.

Title: _____

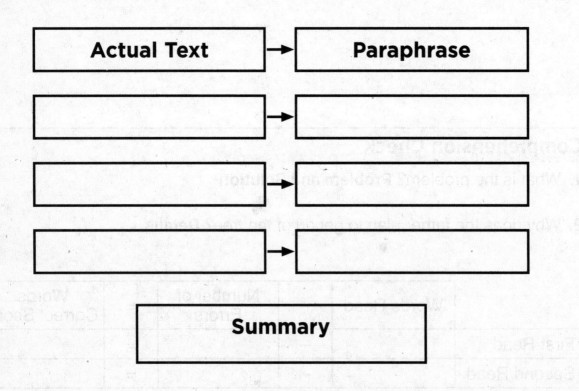

© Macmillan/McGraw-Hill

When an author wants to help a reader see and remember a sequence of events, he or she will often include a **time line**. On a **time line**, events are shown in the order in which they took place.

Use the time line below to answer the questions.

1821: Mexico wins independence from Spain.

1850: California becomes the 31st state.

1769: First European settlement is founded in San Diego.

1846: Mexican-American War begins.

| 1750 | 1770 | 1790 | 1810 | 1830 | 1850 |

1781: Los Angeles founded.

1848: Mexican-American War ends; California joins U.S.

1. Which is the first event shown on the time line?

_____

2. When did Mexico win independence from Spain?

_____

3. When did the Mexican-American War begin?

_____

4. About how long did the Mexican-American War last?

_____

5. When did California become a state?

_____

A **thesaurus** is a dictionary of **synonyms,** words that have almost the same meaning. If you are looking for just the right word, a thesaurus can help you find it.

Read this thesaurus entry. Then answer the questions below.

delight
noun
synonyms: happiness, gladness, joy, pleasure

1. What part of speech is *delight*?

   _____

2. What is another word that has almost the same meaning as *delight*?

   _____

3. Use the word *delight* in a sentence.

   _____

4. Write the sentence again, this time using a synonym for *delight*.

   _____

5. How would you find another word that means almost the same as *explore*?

   _____

Name _____

A. Reading Strategy: Summarize and Paraphrase

Summarizing and paraphrasing information and ideas from texts will help you understand what you read. When you summarize and paraphrase, keep the meaning of the text clear. Also, include information from the text in an order that makes sense. Choose a text that you are reading this week, and complete the activity.

Use this chart to paraphrase a key idea from the text.

Actual Text	Paraphrase

Use this chart to summarize part or all of the text.

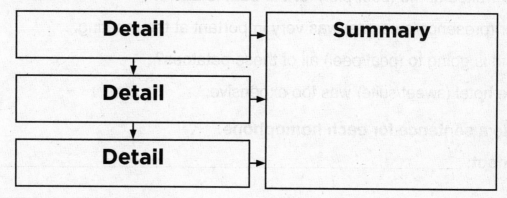

B. Independent Reading Log

Choose something you would like to read. After reading, complete the reading log. Be sure to include the main idea or meaning of the text. Keep the details or events in the proper order. You may use your log to talk to others about what you read.

Genre _____

Title _____

Author _____

This Text Is About _____

> **Homophones** are words that sound alike but that have different spellings and different meanings. For example, the words *flour* and *flower* sound alike, but *flour* is used to make bread, and a *flower* is the bloom of a plant.

A. Choose the word that best completes each sentence. Circle the correct word.

1. They took a (poll/pole) to see which brand of cereal people liked best.

2. She did not like to (waist/waste) time watching television.

3. Dad ate toast with red (current/currant) jelly for breakfast.

4. My aunt is running for city (counsel/council).

5. We waited at the (peer/pier) for the boat to arrive.

6. Her (presence/presents) was very important at the meeting.

7. Who is going to (peal/peel) all of these potatoes?

8. The hotel (sweet/suite) was too expensive.

B. Write a sentence for each homophone.

9. accept: _____

_____

10. except: _____

_____

11. affect: _____

_____

12. effect: _____

_____

Name _____

A. Select the correct vocabulary word from the choices in parentheses. Write the word on the line provided.

1. Horses were important to the cowboy's job. They enabled the cowboy to travel easily over the (vastness, horizon) of the countryside.

   _____

2. The cowboys had great (hunger, enthusiasm) for their job and eagerly helped the rancher herd the cattle. _____

3. Sometimes it seemed as though the horses could ride all the way to the (horizon, vastness), where the land met the sky. _____

4. The (vastness, presence) of the horses helped keep the cattle under control. _____

5. Both cows and horses had to be careful not to slip into a (horizon, ravine). Such a steep, narrow canyon was a danger. _____

6. Horses (suspended, swerved) around the cows to keep the herd moving in the right direction. _____

7. The rattlesnake's rattle made a (distinct, suspended) sound that every cowboy knew. _____

8. The horses slept with the cowboys' spurs (swerved, suspended) from the top of their saddles. _____

B. Write new sentences for two of the vocabulary words used above. Then underline the vocabulary word.

9. _____

   _____

10. _____

    _____

Name _____

> **Making inferences** can help you better understand the
> characters and plot development of a story. You make inferences
> when you connect clues in the story with your own related
> knowledge to figure out information about characters and events
> that are not directly stated in the story.

**Read each passage, then make an inference about the situations
and characters.**

1. Bob Lemmons saw the wild mustangs and pulled the reins to slow his
   horse, Warrior. The mustangs looked up but didn't run.
   Inference: Bob slowed his horse because

   _____

2. Bob was the only cowboy who could get close to the wild horses. They
   accepted him into the herd.
   Inference: Bob's relationship with horses was

   _____

3. The sky darkened, and Bob saw lightning flash around him. He quickly led
   Warrior to a ravine for shelter.
   Inference: Bob and Warrior sought shelter because

   _____

4. The mustang stallion fought Bob and Warrior. Bob guided Warrior's blows
   and the stallion fell, returning meekly to the herd.
   Inference: The leaders of the mustang herd after the fight are

   _____

5. **Analyze your inferences. What do they tell you about Bob's life as a**

   cowboy? _____

   _____

   _____

© Macmillan/McGraw-Hill

Name _____

As you read *Black Cowboy Wild Horses*, fill in the Inferences Chart.

Text Clues	What You Know	Inferences

How does the information you wrote in the Inferences Chart help you
monitor comprehension of *Black Cowboy Wild Horses*?

As I read, I will pay attention to rate.

	Alice was born in 1902 on a ranch near Red Lodge,
11	Montana. Because they traveled on horses, the Greenough
19	family kept dozens of them to ride. Alice also fed cattle,
30	roped them, and rounded them up. She developed the riding
40	and roping skills that would later bring her fame.
49	Alice had seven brothers and sisters, five of whom wound
59	up working in rodeos. They became known as the "Riding
69	Greenoughs." Alice later said, "We learned to ride before we
79	could walk."
81	Ranch life was busy. The family planted, grew, and
90	harvested crops. Cattle had to be rounded up and fed.
100	Someone had to tame the horses and teach them to carry a
112	rider or pull a wagon. In addition, the fences needed fixing,
123	and the buildings and machines needed repairs. 130

Comprehension Check

1. What were some of the chores on the Greenoughs' ranch? **Main Idea and Details**

2. Why do you think five of the Greenoughs ended up working in rodeos? **Plot**

	Words Read	–	Number of Errors	=	Words Correct Score
First Read		–		=	
Second Read		–		=	

© Macmillan/McGraw-Hill

A biography or an autobiography tells about important events in someone's life. Authors often use **literary language** to help readers understand these events. Similes, metaphors, personification, and repetition are kinds of literary language. A simile compares two unlike things. A simile begins with *like* or *as*. A metaphor also compares unlike things, but a metaphor does not include *like* or *as*. The use of personification gives human qualities to nonhuman things. Repetition, or the repeating of a word or phrase, creates rhythm and draws attention to certain ideas.

Read the sentences from the passage. Then complete the items.

He looked down at the corral where the other cowboys were beginning the morning chores and then turned away and stared at the land stretching as wide as love in every direction. The sky was curved as though it were a lap on which the earth lay napping like a curled cat. High above, a hawk was suspended on cold threads of unseen winds. Far, far away, at what looked to be the edge of the world, land and sky kissed.

1. List the three similes from the passage.

   _____

   _____

   _____

2. How do the similes help you understand the event? _____

   _____

   _____

3. Write a metaphor about a hawk from the passage. What comparison does the metaphor make?

   _____

4. Write the example of personification from the passage.

   _____

When you read poetry, pay attention to features often used with poetic language. For example, poems often include **repetition**, which occurs when a line or a sequence of lines appears more than once. **Assonance** is the repetition of the same or similar vowel sounds in a series of words, usually words with different consonant sounds. Repetition and assonance give poems a musical quality and rhythm.

Read the poem. Then answer the questions.

1 There once was a filly named Blaze,
2 Who wouldn't come out of the rain.
3 First that filly got soaked.
4 Then she grew hoarse and croaked,
5 Which put out that filly named Blaze.

1. In which lines do you see repetition? _____

_____

2. What is the example of assonance in the repeated words? _____

_____

3. What other examples of assonance do you see in line 1? _____

_____

4. What is the example of assonance in line 2? _____

_____

5. Is there an example of assonance in line 3? _____

_____

6. Is there an example of assonance in line 4? _____

_____

© Macmillan/McGraw-Hill

An **analogy** is a statement that compares two pairs of words. The relationship between the two words in the first pair is the same as the relationship between the two words in the second pair. **Antonyms**, two words with opposite meanings, can be used in analogies.

| criticize | energetic | absence | soft |

Complete each analogy by providing an appropriate antonym from the box. Then write a sentence using one pair of antonyms from the analogy.

1. feebly is to strongly as tired is to _____

_____

_____

2. presence is to _____ as arrive is to depart

_____

_____

3. light is to heavy as _____ is to hard

_____

_____

4. awake is to asleep as praise is to _____

_____

_____

Analogies can also be used to compare pairs of synonyms. On a separate sheet of paper, write 3 analogies using synonyms.

A. Reading Strategy: Summarize and Paraphrase

Summarizing and paraphrasing information and ideas from texts will help you understand what you read. When you summarize and paraphrase, keep the meaning of the text clear. Also, include information from the text in an order that makes sense. Choose a text that you are reading this week, and complete the chart.

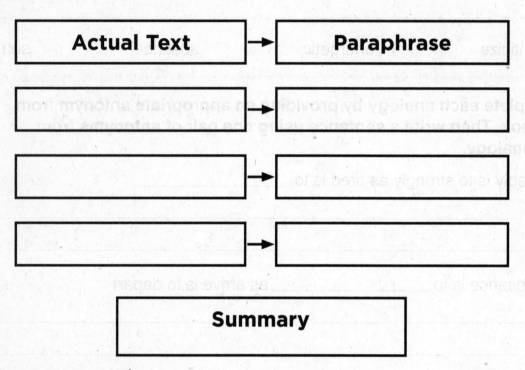

B. Independent Reading Log

Choose something you would like to read. After reading, complete the reading log. Be sure to include the main idea or meaning of the text. Keep the details or events in the proper order. You may use your log to talk to others about what you read.

Genre _____

Title _____

Author _____

This Text Is About _____

_____

© Macmillan/McGraw-Hill

Name _____

A **prefix** is an affix added to the front of a base or root word.
When you add a prefix, you change the meaning of the word.
In- means "without; not."
Dis- means "the opposite or lack of; not."
Mis- means "bad or wrong."
Pre- means "before."

**Add *in-*, *dis-*, *mis-*, or *pre-* to each of the words in the sentences
below. Use context clues to help you decide which prefix to use.**

1. My teacher _____ approves of talking in class because it disturbs
   the other students.

2. A lumpy mattress can cause _____ comfort for your back.

3. You may need to _____ wash new clothes before you wear them.

4. The outfielder _____ judged the fly ball and did not make the catch.

5. You should not _____ judge food before you try it because you
   might actually like it.

6. My father _____ heats the oven before he puts the food in.

7. Rivals often _____ trust each other because they think the other
   person is trying to trick them.

8. The cheap toys were _____ expensive, so Mom agreed to buy them.

9. I _____ understood my teacher and wrote the wrong spelling word.

10. It is _____ honest to cheat on a test.

Choose the correct word that best completes the following sentences. Then write a new sentence with the word.

1. Our teacher tries to (instill/insert) a love of reading in each of us.

   _____

   _____

   _____

2. A (linguist/naturalist) is a person who studies nature. _____

   _____

   _____

3. The (singular/diverse) life in the park included many types of trees and wildlife.

   _____

   _____

   _____

4. We planted a neighborhood garden in the (busy/vacant) lot.

   _____

   _____

   _____

5. We (separated/combined) the soil with sand to help it drain well.

   _____

   _____

   _____

Name _____

A **cause** is an event or action that makes something happen. An **effect** is the result, or the thing that happens. Recognizing cause-and-effect relationships will help you better understand why events in a text happen, what will probably happen next, and how all the events in a text are related.

Match each cause with an effect from the box. Write the letter of the effect on the line provided.

Effects:

a. Lewis and Clark were sent to explore the new territory.

b. received help from friendly Native American tribes.

c. created accurate journals that described people, places, and things.

d. Lewis, Clark, and their team had very little to eat.

e. doubling the size of the United States.

Causes:

1. Lewis and Clark took many breaks to write down everything they saw, which _____.

2. President Jefferson bought the Louisiana Territory from France, thus _____.

3. The buffalo moved south for the winter, so _____.

4. Lewis and Clark did not know the land of the Louisiana Purchase, so they _____.

5. President Jefferson wanted to find a water route to the Pacific Ocean, so _____.

As you read *A Historic Journey*, fill in the Cause and Effect Chart.

Cause	➡	Effect
	➡	
	➡	
	➡	
	➡	

How does the information you wrote in this Cause and Effect Chart help
you make inferences and analyze *A Historic Journey*?

© Macmillan/McGraw-Hill

As I read, I will pay attention to phrasing.

	Nature is amazingly complex. Every day many different
8	things happen in nature. Look around and observe. What do
18	you see happening?
21	Living things grow and die as the seasons change. Even the
32	quietest place is not **vacant**. Insects fill the air. Animals search
43	for food and build their homes. Fish and frogs splash in the
55	water. And nature is so **diverse**, too. There are millions of kinds
67	of plants and animals to study.
73	But learning from nature takes time and patience. And that's
83	especially true of animals.
87	You can't just press a button on a hawk and have it tell you
101	how fast it can fly. And chimps don't wear signs telling you
113	how they take care of their young. To learn these things, you
125	have to observe the animals.
130	The people you'll read about here each observed animals in
140	a different way. And each gave the world something through
150	his observations. Some helped us make sense of the natural
160	world. Others helped us see the importance of protecting it. 170

Comprehension Check

1. What does the word *diverse* mean? **Context Clues**

2. What does it mostly take to learn from nature? **Main Idea and Details**

	Words Read	–	Number of Errors	=	Words Correct Score
First Read		–		=	
Second Read		–		=	

An **organizational pattern** is used by a writer to present information in a way that makes sense to a reader. Writers can use several organizational patterns: cause-and-effect, compare and contrast, sequential order, logical order, and classification schemes. Some reading passages blend types of organization.

Cause-and-effect organization shows why something happened. A passage can begin with a cause and then describe its effects. Or it can begin with an effect that is then traced back to a cause.

Read the last paragraph on page 583 of "A Historic Journey." Then complete the items that follow.

1. Use the information from the paragraph to complete the chart with three effects of the listed cause.

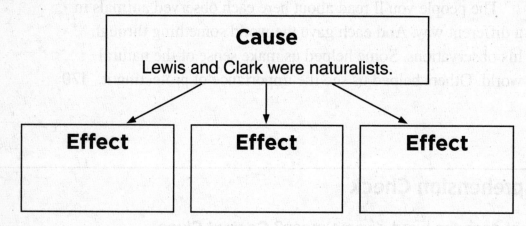

Cause

Lewis and Clark were naturalists.

| Effect | Effect | Effect |

2. How does this organizational pattern help readers understand the relationships among ideas?

_____

_____

_____

_____

Name _____

A **dictionary** entry tells you what a word means and how to pronounce it. It also tells whether a word is a noun, a verb, or another part of speech. A **thesaurus** entry provides a list of words with similar meanings. It also contains parts of speech for each of the words.

Use the sample dictionary and thesaurus entries in the box to answer the questions below.

Dictionary:
na-ture (´nā chər) *n.*: 1. the basic character of a person 2. the physical world, especially living things and objects such as rocks and air

Thesaurus:
Natural: *adj:* normal, typical, regular
Natural: *adj:* inherent, ingrained
Nature: *n:* type, kind

1. How many meanings does the dictionary list for the word *nature*? _____

2. *Ingrained* is another word for _____.

3. Which definition of the word *nature* is the one studied by naturalists? How do you know? _____

_____

4. Write the definition of *nature* that is used in this sentence: *True to her kind nature, the social worker delivered meals to the elderly.* _____

_____

5. What other words might the thesaurus list that mean the same as *nature*?

_____

Antonyms are words with opposite meanings. A thesaurus or dictionary is a tool that can help you find antonyms for a particular word.

A. Read the paragraph. Use a thesaurus to find the antonym from the box for each underlined word.

| diverse | careful | accurate | land | large | revealed |

    Lewis and Clark made a <u>small</u> _____ contribution to exploration. Without them the secrets of the enormous <u>ocean</u> _____ area known as the Louisiana Purchase may have never been <u>hidden</u> _____. Lewis and Clark were the first ones to explore the <u>same</u> _____ regions that make up the United States. They passed through the Great Plains, Badlands, and Rocky Mountains. They were very <u>careless</u> _____ about taking <u>incorrect</u> _____ notes about the people, plants, and animals they came across. With help from friendly Native American tribes, Lewis and Clark made it all the way to the Pacific Ocean.

B. Use the antonym word pairs from above to write four sentences. Underline each antonym.

1. _____

2. _____

3. _____

4. _____

A. Reading Strategy: Summarize and Paraphrase

Summarizing and paraphrasing information and ideas from texts will help you understand what you read. When you summarize and paraphrase, keep the meaning of the text clear. Also, include information from the text in an order that makes sense. Choose a text that you are reading this week, and complete the chart.

Paraphrases	Summary

B. Independent Reading Log

Choose something you would like to read. After reading, complete the reading log. Be sure to include the main idea or meaning of the text. Keep the details or events in the proper order. You may use your log to talk to others about what you read.

Genre _____

Title _____

Author _____

This Text Is About _____

_____

_____

Suffixes are word parts that are added to the end of words to change their meanings. The suffix *-less* means "without." The suffix *-ness* means "the state or act of."

When added to base words, the suffixes *-less* and *-ness* are unaccented syllables. They receive less stress than the base words.

Example: fond + *-ness* = fondness. *Fond* is the accented syllable, while the suffix *-ness* is unaccented.

Use what you know about suffixes to write the meanings of the words in the chart. Then write the words in syllables. Write the accented syllable in capital letters. Follow the example.

Base word + suffix	Meaning	Accented syllable
Example: fearless	without fear, brave	FEAR less
effortless		
fierceness		
stillness		
forgiveness		
meaningless		
harmless		
weakness		
weightlessness		
motionless		
gladness		

A. Choose a word from the box to complete each sentence.

impress	wring	posed	original
commenced	advertisement	elected	sauntered

1. I just saw an _____ for a new book about Davy Crockett.

2. Davy Crockett packed his bag and _____ his trip.

3. Davy Crockett could easily _____ people because he could do so many things.

4. Davy Crockett had to _____ a dead limb off a big oak tree.

5. Davy Crockett _____ for a picture with the President.

6. He was _____ to Congress when he received more votes than anyone else.

7. I _____ back to the library, thinking about Davy Crockett as I strolled along.

8. The _____ tall tale about Davy Crockett was told in the 1800s.

B. Write new sentences for two of the vocabulary words used above. Then underline the vocabulary word.

9. _____

_____

10. _____

_____

The **plot** is the series of related events in a story. In some stories, the plot includes a problem that a character must solve. The **setting** is where and when the story takes place. The setting can influence or affect events in the plot.

Read the tall tale below. Identify the setting and the events in the plot.

When a speeding comet threatened to crash into Earth, everyone turned to Davy Crockett for help. Davy Crockett was the biggest, strongest, most courageous man alive. If anyone could save Earth, Davy Crockett could!

Everyone gathered around Davy as he prepared to climb the tallest mountain in Texas. "I'll hop right up to the top of this mountain," he exclaimed, "and grab that comet by the tail. I'll toss it away quicker than you can say 'howdy-do.'"

The people held their breath as Davy took long strides up the mountain. His legs were a blur because they moved so quickly. The crowd gasped when Davy disappeared into the clouds. Would Davy stop the comet?

Just then, the crowd jumped back with a loud roar. Davy had grabbed the comet's tail. He twirled the comet around like a lasso and then sent it flying into outer space.

Davy hadn't even begun to sweat! Davy Crockett proved once again that there was nothing he couldn't do.

Summary: _____

_____

_____

_____

_____

_____

As you read *Davy Crockett Saves the World*, fill in the Plot and Setting Chart.

Plot	Setting

How does the information you wrote in this Plot and Setting Chart help you analyze the story structure of *Davy Crockett Saves the World*?

© Macmillan/McGraw-Hill

Name _____

As I read, I will pay attention to my expression.

	Back then it wasn't easy to feed a large family. Luckily
11	Johnny possessed a green thumb. From the time that he was
22	two years old, it seemed as if Johnny could just look at
34	a seed and a plant commenced to grow. So Johnny and his
46	green thumb fed his large family.
52	There was plenty of food, but dinnertime was extremely
61	noisy in Johnny's house. Why, it was as if a volcano was
73	exploding at dinnertime! As soon as the food hit the table,
84	the children shouted and complained.
89	"Tommy's apple pie is bigger than mine!"
96	"Why are we having apple juice again?"
103	All that noise gave Johnny a headache, so he would take
114	his dinner outside and escape to his favorite spot, the apple
125	orchard. There, Johnny felt at home. 131

Comprehension Check

1. What kind of person was Johnny? **Character**

2. How did Johnny's family benefit from his green thumb? **Plot**

	Words Read	–	Number of Errors	=	Words Correct Score
First Read		–		=	
Second Read		–		=	

© Macmillan/McGraw-Hill

The **theme** of a work of literature is the message or lesson that a writer wants to share. Some works of literature are based on historical events or movements. The themes of these works often explore the life lessons learned from the events and the people who actually experienced them.

Read the short biography of the real Davy Crockett below. Then complete the items that follow.

Davy Crockett was an American frontiersman who was born in Tennessee in 1786. At the age of 12, he worked for a cattle driver. When Davy's contract ended, the cattle driver refused to let him go, so Davy escaped from the man during a snowstorm. Davy Crockett served as a soldier during the War of 1812. In 1821, he was elected to the Tennessee legislature. He also served in the U.S. Congress from 1827 to 1831 and from 1833 to 1835. In Washington, Crockett became famous for his frontier clothing, humor, and tall tales. After losing an election in November 1835, Crockett moved to Texas, where he was killed at the Alamo in March 1836.

1. Compare the real Davy Crockett with the character Davy in the story "Davy Crockett Saves the World." _____

_____

2. Contrast the real Davy Crockett with the character from the story.

_____

_____

_____

_____

3. What effect does the life of the real Davy Crockett have on the theme of the story "Davy Crockett Saves the World"? _____

_____

_____

Name _____

A **toolbar** is a strip of symbols that allows you to do specific actions
with a Web page or document. A **link** is an electronic connection on
a Web site that provides direct access to other information.

Use the Web site page to answer the questions.

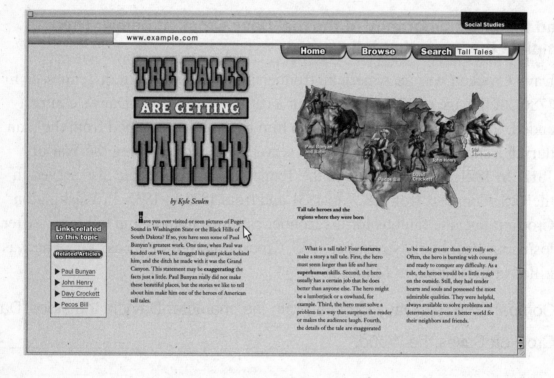

1. Why is the toolbar important? _____

_____

_____

2. What do links do? _____

_____

3. On this Web site, how else would you get information on tall tales?

_____

_____

© Macmillan/McGraw-Hill

Sometimes two smaller words are put together to form a **compound word**. Recognizing the smaller words can help you figure out the compound word's meaning. For example, *newspaper* is a compound word made from the words *news* and *paper*. The word *newspaper* means "paper on which news is published."

Underline the compound word in each sentence. Then use the meaning of smaller words to help you write the compound word's meaning.

1. The storyteller told an exciting tale about Davy Crockett. _____

_____

2. One story is about how Pecos Bill tames a whirlwind. _____

_____

3. I wrote a story about Sluefoot Sue in my notebook. _____

_____

4. The townspeople decided to ask Davy Crockett for help. _____

_____

5. We could see for miles from the top of the skyscraper. _____

_____

6. For dinner, Davy Crockett ate homegrown tomatoes in his salad. _____

_____

7. Today we will cut the grass with our electric lawnmower. _____

_____

8. I bought some groceries and a magazine from the shopkeeper. _____

_____

A. Reading Strategy: Summarize and Paraphrase

Summarizing and paraphrasing information and ideas from texts will help you understand what you read. When you summarize and paraphrase, keep the meaning of the text clear. Also, include information from the text in an order that makes sense. Choose a text that you are reading this week, and complete the activity.

Paraphrase three key ideas from a section of the text.

Paraphrase 1: _____

_____

Paraphrase 2: _____

_____

Paraphrase 3: _____

_____

Use your paraphrases to summarize that section of the text.

_____

_____

_____

B. Independent Reading Log

Choose something you would like to read. After reading, complete the reading log. Be sure to include the main idea or meaning of the text. Keep the details or events in the proper order. You may use your log to talk to others about what you read.

Genre _____

Title _____

Author _____

This Text Is About _____

_____

_____

The suffix *-ion* means "act or process", or "state or condition." You must drop the **e** from words that end in silent **e** before adding *-ion*. For example, the word **separate** must lose its **e** before you can add *-ion* to make the word **separation**.

Add *-ion* to the words in the box to complete each sentence below. Remember to drop the silent e before adding *-ion*.

concentrate	exhaust	confuse	discuss
elect	decorate	correct	locate

1. The results of the _____ showed that the more experienced candidate won the most votes.

2. The incomplete directions led to _____ among the students.

3. They used the roses as _____ on the parade float.

4. He was so focused during the test that nothing could break his

   _____ .

5. Staying up late can lead to _____ if you do not get enough sleep.

6. Although the _____ of the park was marked on the map, she could not find it.

7. The student worked very hard on his paper, and it needed only one small

   _____ .

8. When they could not agree, their _____ quickly became an argument.

**Choose a vocabulary word from the choices in parentheses.
Then write the correct word on the line provided.**

1. I will write a letter to my (representative/attorney) in Congress about this
   problem. _____

2. (Colonel/Physician) is one of the highest ranks among the officers in the
   army. _____

3. A few people had the (submit/notion) that women should have the right
   to vote. _____

4. To (submit/qualify) as a voter, you must be at least 18 years old.
   _____

5. Congress is still debating, so they will delay, or (submit/postpone), the vote
   until next week. _____

6. She knew that the old law was not (satisfactory/escorted) for today.
   _____

7. When we finish writing, we can (submit/qualify) our letters to our
   representatives. _____

8. Our (attorney/physician) will present our case to the judge.
   _____

© Macmillan/McGraw-Hill

Name _____

A **fact** is a statement that can be proven true. An **opinion** is a statement that a person believes, but that cannot be proven true. A **relevant detail** is an important piece of information that may be either a fact or an opinion. A relevant detail should relate to the other ideas in the text and help you make inferences and draw conclusions about the text.

Use information from "When Esther Morris Headed West" to decide whether each statement below is a fact or an opinion. Write your choice in the box next to each sentence. Then explain each of your decisions, and whether the fact or opinion is a relevant detail.

Statement	Fact or Opinion	Explanation of Decision
Esther Morris was a very smart person.		
Benjamin Sheeks thought that women's suffrage was hogwash.		
In 1869, the Wyoming legislature voted to give the women of Wyoming the vote.		
The people who lived in Wyoming in 1869 were pleasant.		
Esther ran for office after women in Wyoming got the vote.		
After Esther Morris was elected, she did a good job as justice of the peace.		

Name _____

**As you read *When Esther Morris Headed West*, fill in the
Fact and Opinion Chart.**

Fact	Opinion

How does the information you wrote in the Fact and Opinion Chart help
you generate questions about *When Esther Morris Headed West*?

Name _____

As I read, I will pay attention to accuracy.

	The fight for women's rights started with the fight to end
11	slavery. Beginning in the 1820s, many women became active
19	in the struggle for the abolition (ab-uh-LISH-uhn), or end,
27	of slavery.
29	One woman who worked hard to fight slavery was
38	Lucretia Mott. In 1833, she started a women's antislavery
46	society in Philadelphia. She went to London to attend the
56	first World's Anti-Slavery Convention. Women had to sit
64	behind a curtain. They couldn't be seen or heard. Lucretia
74	Mott was furious.
77	Also attending the London convention was Elizabeth
84	Cady Stanton. She, too, was angry at the limited role that
95	women were allowed. She and Mott became friends. Mott
104	was some 20 years older, but they shared many of the
114	same views.
116	The two friends began to talk with other women who
126	were working to free the slaves. They talked about how hard
137	women's lives were. They talked about the need to make
147	changes. They talked about how they might work together to
157	fight for their own rights. 162

Comprehension Check

1. What does the word *abolition* mean? **Context Clues**

2. How did Lucretia Mott fight to end slavery? **Main Idea and Details**

	Words Read	−	Number of Errors	=	Words Correct Score
First Read		−		=	
Second Read		−		=	

© Macmillan/McGraw-Hill

Authors of biographies and autobiographies often use literary devices such as **dialect** to help readers imagine another person's life. Dialect is a way of speaking that is common to a particular group of people. A dialect may be identified by the group's colorful use of words or by the way in which the group arranges or pronounces words. Dialect helps readers visualize the time period and the geographic region in which another person lived.

Read the passage from "When Esther Morris Headed West." Find examples of dialect. Then complete the chart, and answer the questions.

Now that women had the right to vote, it was time to prove that they could hold office just as well. Mrs. Morris had no hankering for power or highfalutin titles. But she knew an idea—even one voted into law—wasn't worth a hill of beans as long as it stayed words on a page. Her boys were grown and it was time to step away from her cooking and gardening for a spell and do a thing that might help women coming along later on.

Examples of Dialect	Meaning

• How does the use of dialect help you understand the biography?

_____

_____

Name _____

A **time line** is a diagram of several events arranged in the order in which they took place. A time line helps to arrange information in an easy, visual way.

Important Events in the Women's Suffrage Movement

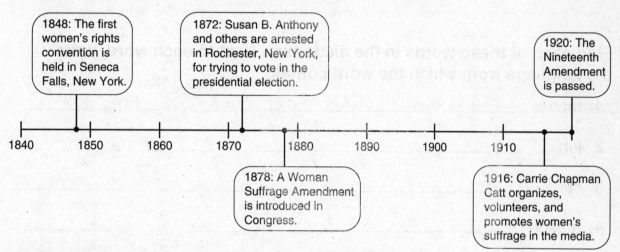

1848: The first women's rights convention is held in Seneca Falls, New York.

1872: Susan B. Anthony and others are arrested in Rochester, New York, for trying to vote in the presidential election.

1920: The Nineteenth Amendment is passed.

1840   1850   1860   1870   1880   1890   1900   1910

1878: A Woman Suffrage Amendment is introduced in Congress.

1916: Carrie Chapman Catt organizes, volunteers, and promotes women's suffrage in the media.

Use the time line to answer the following questions:

1. What is this time line about? _____

_____

2. How many years does the time line cover? _____

3. What happened in 1872? _____

_____

4. Where was the first women's rights conference in the United States held?

_____

5. Who traveled across America to organize volunteers?

_____

6. Which happened first: Seneca Falls Convention or the Nineteenth

Amendment is ratified? _____

Dictionaries are used to find meanings, parts of speech, pronunciation, and syllabication of words, but you can also use a dictionary when you want to check **word origins**. The definition may include information about the word's beginnings or how it has changed over time. It also may tell which language a word comes from or how or when a word became part of the English language.

Find each of these words in the dictionary. Next to each word, write the language from which the word comes.

1. taco _____

2. junk _____

3. car _____

4. reason _____

5. magenta _____

6. tortilla _____

7. city _____

8. dollar _____

9. guitar _____

10. cereal _____

11. music _____

12. radius _____

© Macmillan/McGraw-Hill

Name _____

A. Reading Strategy: Summarize and Paraphrase

Summarizing and paraphrasing information and ideas from texts will help you understand what you read. When you summarize and paraphrase, keep the meaning of the text clear. Also, include information from the text in an order that makes sense. Choose a text that you are reading this week, and complete the chart.

Title
Paraphrase three key ideas.
Paraphrase 1:
Paraphrase 2:
Paraphrase 3:
Use your paraphrases to summarize.

B. Independent Reading Log

Choose something you would like to read. After reading, complete the reading log. Be sure to include the main idea or meaning of the text. Keep the details or events in the proper order. You may use your log to talk to others about what you read.

Genre _____

Title _____

Author _____

This Text Is About _____

_____

_____

Many words have their origin in the Greek language. Word roots are word parts that usually can't stand on their own. Knowing the meanings of **Greek roots** can help you define unfamiliar words.

Read the chart. Then write a word from the box below to complete each sentence correctly.

Greek root	Meaning	Example
astr	star	astronaut
auto	self, same	automatic
photo	light	photogenic
mech	machine	mechanism
graph	thing written	graphic
phon	sound, voice	phonetic
meter	measure	thermometer

photocopy	astronomer	automobile
biography	mechanic	phonics

1. The vehicle needed a _____ who knew how its engine worked.

2. We studied sounds and syllables in our _____ class.

3. Ms. Brown made one more _____ of the worksheet for the new student.

4. The author wrote a _____ about Harriet Tubman.

5. Thanks to the _____, we don't have to walk to school.

6. An _____ looked at the stars through her telescope.

A. Select the best word from the choices in parentheses. Then write the correct word on the line provided.

1. Have you seen the (categories, corners) of talents that will be allowed at the talent contest? _____

2. Did you see the size of the stage? It's (slow, gigantic)! _____

3. We walked to the contest in the rain, and now our clothes are (soggy, dry). _____

4. The man was tired, so he (slumped, sat up) in his chair and went to sleep. _____

5. Cynthia twisted (blocks, strands) of hair around her finger. _____

6. If we write a paper, will Mr. Price give us extra (credit, time)? _____

7. Our school has lights in front of the stage, so all of the performers have a (luminous, dark) glow on their faces. _____

8. All of the performers were quite (splendid, capable) of putting on a good show. _____

B. Write new sentences for two of the vocabulary words used above. Then underline the vocabulary word.

9. _____

_____

10. _____

_____

Name _____

> The **characters** are the people or animals in a story. The **plot** is
> a series of events that take the characters through an experience,
> change, or a problem that a character has to solve. The relationships
> and characteristics of the characters influence the events of the plot.

Read the passage and answer the questions below.

    Tuesday, I caught a bad cold and had to stay home from school. The next
day was Wednesday, and Mrs. Mandle always assigned an essay that day.
That afternoon I called my best friend, Roberto. He is a great writer and
listens carefully to Mrs. Mandle's essay questions. However, when I called
Roberto, his voice was muffled and what he said wasn't very clear.

    "Mike," Roberto said, "the essay is on 'what makes blueberry pies.'"

    "What?" I said. "The essay is on 'what makes blueberry pies'?"

    "Yes," he said. "I hope you feel butter. I have to go to digger now."

    That night I wrote about blueberry pies and how to make them. The
next day I felt better and went to school. I saw Roberto and talked about my
blueberry pie essay.

    "Blueberry pies?" Roberto asked. "We didn't have to write about
blueberry pies. Our essay was about 'what makes blue skies.'"

1. Who are the characters in this passage? _____

_____

2. What is Mike's main problem? _____

_____

3. Why does Mike call Roberto for the essay question? _____

_____

_____

4. What could Mike have done differently to solve his essay problem?

_____

_____

Name _____

As you read *Miss Alaineus*, fill in the Character and Plot Chart.

Character	Plot

How does the information you wrote in this Character and Plot Chart
help you generate questions about *Miss Alaineus*?

Name _____

As I read, I will pay attention to expression and phrasing.

	Freddy slapped the table as he snorted. "Check this out,
10	Eva!" he said between chuckles.
15	Freddy grabbed my sketchbook and held it up next to my
26	startled face. Eva frowned, looked confused, and then finally
35	a gigantic smile crossed her face.
41	"You're good, Nadia," she said. "But I don't get it."
51	What I'd drawn was a cartoon of *me*, with an oversized
62	head and tiny body. I'd added my trademark features.
71	A banner at the top read "Science UN-Fair." Question marks
81	spun around my head, and I had a very confused look—a
93	perfect caricature, I might add.
98	Freddy turned to me and said, "Eva was in the nurse's
109	office during fifth period. Remember? She got hurt playing
118	soccer during lunch."
121	"Oh, yeah," I said. And then I told Eva what she had
133	missed. 134

Comprehension Check

1. Who is the main character of this story? **Character**

2. What did Nadia draw in her sketchbook? **Plot**

	Words Read	–	Number of Errors	=	Words Correct Score
First Read		–		=	
Second Read		–		=	

© Macmillan/McGraw-Hill

The **theme** of a literary work is the moral lesson that the writer wants to teach. Themes are revealed in the characters' relationships, or how they interact with one another. Sometimes characters have **conflicts**, or disagreements. At other times, characters are friendly. Readers can learn important lessons from both kinds of relationships.

Read the fable. Then answer the questions to compare and contrast the fable with the story "Miss Alaineus."

A donkey found a lion's hide and dressed himself in it. He thought it would be fun to fool the people and the other animals in his village. When the people and the other animals saw him, they ran away in fear that such a fierce beast would attack them. The donkey was so proud of himself that he opened his mouth and let out an enormous bray that echoed through the valley. The people and the other animals started laughing because they had expected a loud roar. "We were afraid of a ferocious lion, but you are only a donkey, so we are not afraid anymore," they said as they returned to the village. With that, the donkey's owner led the embarrassed animal back to the stable.

1. How is the donkey in the fable similar to Sage in the story "Miss Alaineus"?

_____

2. How are the donkey and Sage different? _____

_____

3. What role does pride have in both stories? _____

_____

_____

_____

4. How do the lessons of the stories differ? _____

_____

_____

Name _____

Photographs or drawings provide a visual image of what is happening in the story. **Captions** help explain what the photographs or drawings are about.

Look at the drawing and read the caption. Then answer the questions.

Fifth-graders learn about fitness and health by running a one-mile race.

1. What does the drawing show? _____
_____
_____

2. What other information do you learn from the caption? _____
_____
_____

© Macmillan/McGraw-Hill

Name _____

You can learn the meaning of an unfamiliar word by using the words around it as context clues. Look at the words that appear near the word that you don't know, and try to find a **synonym** of that word to help you figure out its meaning. Remember that a synonym is a word with a similar meaning.

Circle the synonym of the underlined word in each sentence.

1. The size of the hot-air balloon <u>decreased</u> and diminished as air was let out of it.

2. The awful sound was <u>unbearable</u> and it woke me up.

3. The roses <u>flourished</u> and thrived more than any other plant in Mrs. Lyon's garden.

4. It can be <u>hazardous</u> to play near a downed power line because electric currents are dangerous.

5. Chris was modest about winning his national award because he is <u>humble</u>.

6. The <u>extravagant</u> party had circus performers, an orchestra, and chefs. Bob thought it was too expensive for only a few guests.

7. The letter was <u>anonymous</u>, so the sender is unknown.

8. The basketball team returned <u>victorious</u> because they had won the state championship.

9. The teachers said soda is <u>prohibited</u> because bottles are forbidden in the gym.

10. The paper towel will soak up the spilled milk because it will <u>absorb</u> all the moisture.

A. Reading Strategy: Make Connections

You can make connections between or among texts of different genres. Choose a text that you are reading this week. Complete the chart by connecting that text with a text of a different genre.

	Text A	Text B
Genre		
Main Idea/ Theme		
Author's Purpose		
Author's Perspective		
Connections Between the Texts		

B. Independent Reading Log

Choose something you would like to read. After reading, complete the reading log. Be sure to include the main idea or meaning of the text. Keep the details or events in the proper order. You may use your log to talk to others about what you read.

Genre _____

Title _____

Author _____

This Text Is About _____

_____

_____

_____

_____

Many words in English have **Latin roots**. You can define
unfamiliar words by recognizing a Latin root and using context
clues. For example, *scrib* means to write, *rupt* means to break,
ject means to throw, and *dict* means to say.

Latin Roots	Meaning
aud	to hear
tract	to drag, draw
port	to carry
spect	to look
mit/miss	to send

**Read the root chart, and write the root of each underlined word in
the sentences below. Then use context clues and the meaning of
the Latin roots to write a definition of each underlined word.**

1. Making a campfire is tricky. First, an adult must <u>transport</u> wood

   to your campsite. _____ *Transport* means _____.

2. Then you must <u>inspect</u> the wood to make sure that it is dry. _____

   Inspect means _____.

3. When an adult lights the fire, you will notice an <u>audible</u> *crackle* and *pop* as

   the wood begins to burn. _____ *Audible* means _____.

4. The <u>spectacle</u> of a roaring fire is a wonderful sight. _____

   Spectacle means _____.

5. For some people, the main <u>attraction</u> of a campfire is roasting

   marshmallows. _____ *Attraction* means _____

   _____.

A. In the sentences below, circle *correct* if the boldface vocabulary word is used properly. If it is not used correctly, circle *incorrect*.

1. The athlete **wearily** ran across the finish line in record time.

   correct   Incorrect

2. We had a **jubilant**, joyful celebration on New Year's Eve.

   correct   incorrect

3. It took almost 4 hours to **abruptly** bake the cake.

   correct   incorrect

4. After the building collapsed, the streets were covered with **debris**, dust, and pieces of brick.

   correct   incorrect

5. I need something to drink because my throat is **parched**, absolutely dry.

   correct   incorrect

6. Jamaal folded up the **sensation** and mailed it to his sister.

   correct   incorrect

B. Write a sentence for each vocabulary word below.

7. **suspicious** _____

   _____

8. **frayed** _____

   _____

Characters will often face a **problem** throughout a story. Their
efforts to **solve** this problem make up the events of the plot.
By recognizing the problem and solution, you will be able to
summarize the story and you will learn more about the characters.

**Read each passage below. On the lines provided, write the problem
and solution in each passage.**

1. Ellen couldn't think of a new hobby. Her mother said that she should
   seriously consider bird-watching. First of all, it involves spending time
   outdoors. Many trips are planned with groups of people, so bird-watching
   is a good way to make new friends. Best of all, there are many interesting
   birds to see.

   Problem: _____

   Solution: _____

2. I frantically called to my dog Frisky, but it was already too late. She had
   spotted the skunk and was running after it happily. Frisky just wanted to
   play, but the skunk didn't know that. As the skunk lifted its tail, Frisky leaned
   down to get a sniff, and the skunk sprayed her right in the face. Poor Frisky!
   And poor me! I had to give her a bath.

   Problem: _____

   Solution: _____

3. I love watching the butterflies in my garden. Monarch butterflies are
   so pretty. I tried to catch some one day so I could see them up close,
   but I didn't know how. I tried just using my hands, but they damaged
   the butterflies' delicate wings. I tried using a jar, but the butterflies hurt
   themselves by flying against the sides. The next day though, I used a net. It
   was soft enough that it didn't hurt the butterflies. It worked perfectly!

   Problem: _____

   _____

   Solution: _____

Name _____

As you read *Bravo, Tavo!*, fill in the Problem and Solution Chart.

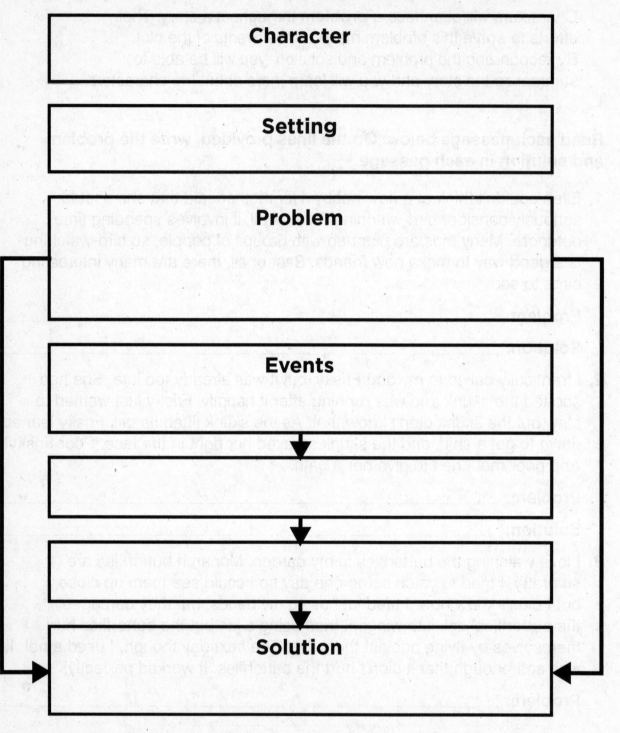

Character

Setting

Problem

Events

Solution

How does the information you wrote in the Problem and Solution Chart help you monitor comprehension of *Bravo, Tavo!*?

As I read, I will pay attention to intonation.

	Lizards, turtles, and snakes are all reptiles. They live in
10	a world full of danger. Predators are on the prowl, looking
21	to eat reptiles that aren't careful. Animals may try to steal
32	their territory or their eggs, or eat them. Reptiles aren't
42	helpless, though. They have many defenses they can use to
52	protect themselves and their homes.
57	In the face of a threat, a reptile's usual behavior is to avoid
70	it. Lizards dart away. Snakes slither away. Turtles hide in
80	their shells or slip into the water. Escape is sometimes the
91	only way to live another day. Often, though, staying out of
102	trouble isn't possible. That's when a reptile uses its defenses
112	to help it stay alive. It may use color, size, special body parts,
125	or even deadly poison to survive. Read on to learn more.
136	Sometimes a reptile can't run away from danger. Most
145	will then try to scare the predator away. Some change the
156	way they stand. Others change the way they look. 165

Comprehension Check

1. What special defenses may reptiles use? **Details**

2. What is this passage mostly about? **Main Idea and Details**

	Words Read	–	Number of Errors	=	Words Correct Score
First Read		–		=	
Second Read		–		=	

Writers use organizational patterns to help readers follow
and understand the text. The pattern of logical order allows
information to flow from one idea to the next in a clear and
consistent way. For example, details in a description may follow a
path from left to right. The writer may also use **headings** to show
the reader what each part of the text is about. This is helpful in
locating information within the text.

Read the passage. Then answer the questions.

Welcome to historic Hunter's Lodge!

History

This lovely hotel was built in 1904 on 60 acres of land. Originally a small
cabin, it was later expanded to accommodate more than 100 guests.

Lobby

The large fireplace to the left of the entrance was once used to cook meals
for guests. It is now a gathering place for storytellers and guests. Just beyond
the fireplace is the general store. To the right of the general store is the main
desk. The doors to the patio are next to the main desk. The passage to the
dining room is on the other side of the patio doors.

Dining Room

The dining room opens at 6 A.M. and serves guests until 9 P.M. Josh Sisler, who
lived in the hotel for ten years, painted the murals on the dining room walls.
Prints of the murals may be purchased in the general store. A list of the hotel's
famous guests, which includes several presidents, is posted in the lobby.

1. What purpose do the headings serve?

   _____

2. In what order does the writer describe the lobby?

   _____

3. Which information in the Dining Room section belongs in the Lobby section?

   Explain your answer. _____

   _____

© Macmillan/McGraw-Hill

Name _____

A **diagram** uses words and pictures to show how people, things, or ideas are connected.

A **heading** is a subtitle that helps readers organize information so it is easier to understand.

This diagram shows how plants make their own food by a process called photosynthesis. Study the diagram. Use it to answer the questions below.

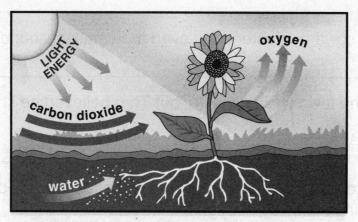

The Process of Photosynthesis

1. What three things does a plant need? _____

_____

2. What is this diagram about according to the heading? _____

_____

3. How does water enter a plant? _____

_____

4. What does a plant release into the air during photosynthesis? ___

_____

You can define an unknown word by using **context clues**, the words around an unknown word that give you clues to the word's meaning.

Circle the context clues in each sentence that can help you figure out the meaning of the underlined word. Then write the definition of the underlined word on the line.

1. The skunk, <u>unaware</u> how bad Tina smelled after spraying her, walked away as if nothing happened.

   unaware: _____

2. The hiker was a <u>coward,</u> frightened at even the smallest sound.

   coward: _____

3. The <u>location</u> of the town was unknown, but Tom believed he knew where the place was.

   location: _____

4. The boat had a tough time <u>navigating</u> the rough seas, but the dolphins had no problem making their way through the waves.

   navigating: _____

5. The thornbug's camouflage was <u>flawless</u>, a perfect disguise that amazed the students.

   flawless: _____

6. He was so <u>grouchy</u> after being sprayed by the skunk that nothing could change his grumpy mood.

   grouchy: _____

7. The <u>pesky</u> mosquito annoyed the girl as it buzzed in her ear.

   pesky: _____

8. The cliffs marked the southern <u>boundary</u> of the village, and the river marked the northern edge.

   boundary: _____

© Macmillan/McGraw-Hill

Name _____

A. Reading Strategy: Make Connections

You can make connections between or among texts of different genres. Choose a text that you are reading this week. Complete the chart by connecting that text with a text of a different genre. Concentrate on making connections about main idea/theme, author's purpose, or author's perspective.

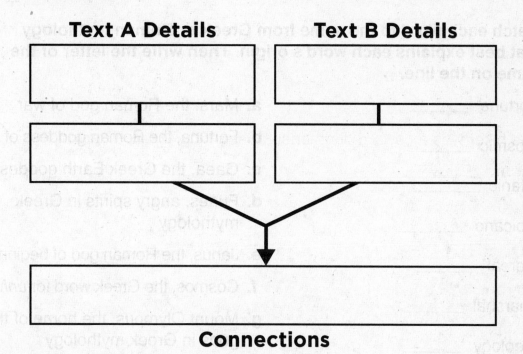

Text A Details   **Text B Details**

Connections

B. Independent Reading Log

Choose something you would like to read. After reading, complete the reading log. Be sure to include the main idea or meaning of the text. Keep the details or events in the proper order. You may use your log to talk to others about what you read.

Genre _____

Title _____

Author _____

This Text Is About _____

_____

The origins of many English words are the names of characters from Greek and Roman mythology. Recognizing **words from mythology** can help you figure out the meanings of some unfamiliar words.

A. Match each word to the name from Greek or Roman mythology that best explains each word's origin. Then write the letter of the name on the line.

1. fortune _____

2. cosmic _____

3. titanic _____

4. volcano _____

5. cereal _____

6. marshal _____

7. geology _____

8. furious _____

9. January _____

10. Olympics _____

a. Mars, the Roman god of war

b. Fortuna, the Roman goddess of luck

c. Gaea, the Greek Earth goddess

d. Furies, angry spirits in Greek mythology

e. Janus, the Roman god of beginnings

f. Cosmos, the Greek word for *universe*

g. Mount Olympus, the home of the gods in Greek mythology

h. Titans, Greek giants who had enormous strength

i. Ceres, the Roman goddess of grain

j. Vulcan, the Roman god of fire

B. Use four words from the first column to make two sentences.

11. _____

_____

12. _____

_____

© Macmillan/McGraw-Hill

Name _____

A. Match the words with their definitions. Then write the letter on the line.

1. rigid _____
2. wheelchair _____
3. interact _____
4. physical _____
5. elementary _____

a. of or relating to the body
b. not yielding or bending
c. simple or basic
d. a chair mounted on wheels
e. to act on or influence each other

B. Choose the word in parentheses that will complete each sentence. Then write the word on the line.

6. Children should learn (physical, rigid) activities that they will still enjoy

   when they are adults. _____

7. Sports that allow you to (salute, interact) with the natural environment are

   exciting. _____

8. The team followed a (rigid, gracious) exercise routine that involved running
   a mile, doing 100 push-ups, and jumping rope every day.

   _____

9. A person in a (parasol, wheelchair) can compete in the Paralympics.

   _____

10. Pete was new to sailing, so he took an (elementary, diverse) sailing class

    to learn more. _____

C. Find the vocabulary words in the word search below.

11. j u w o i c s p h y s i c a l l k j
12. a k j e l e m e n t a r y u e u y p
13. r i g y i u o w h e e l c h a i r z
14. a r l r i g i d l k j j f i n t e r

Persuasion is communication meant to convince you of an opinion that is the author's viewpoint. Authors can use a variety of persuasive techniques, including:

• **Testimonial:** A noteworthy person supports a product.
• **Bandwagon:** The product or activity is said to be popular with everyone. This is exaggerated and contradictory; there is no reason to advertise something that is popular with everyone.
• **Emotional appeal:** Language used to make a person feel strong emotions. This is misleading since it plays off emotions instead of reason.
• **Repetition:** A product or service name is repeated many times.
• **Slogan:** A catchy phrase is used to sell a product.

A. Match a technique of persuasion to each example.

1. Our wheelchairs are used by all Paralympians everywhere.

   _____

2. Boundless Playgrounds are fun! Boundless Playgrounds are safe! Boundless Playgrounds make memories! _____

3. A GWPAS device makes you "Glad to Walk Positively Anywhere Safely."

   _____

4. Because of FastBreak Wheelchairs, I was named one of the top young athletes in the nation. _____

5. Would you enjoy never going anywhere new, never hearing new sounds, and never meeting new people? Probably not. With navigation, you can be free to walk anywhere, any way, and any time that you want!

   _____

B. Work with a partner. Choose one example. Discuss the author's position in the example. Write another example, using a different viewpoint.

© Macmillan/McGraw-Hill

Name _____

As you read "A Dream Comes True," fill in the Fact and Opinion Chart.

Fact	Opinion

How does the information you wrote in this Fact and Opinion Chart help you monitor comprehension of "A Dream Comes True"?

Name _____

As I read, I will pay attention to accuracy.

7	**Wheelchair** basketball is probably the oldest competitive wheelchair sport. It began after World War II as a way to get
19	disabled veterans active. Now children ages six and up are
29	playing wheelchair basketball in gyms everywhere. They
36	play on the same size court and use most of the same rules as
50	their classmates. And they're getting a lot of exercise, too.
60	Only a few rules are adapted in wheelchair basketball.
69	For example, if a player takes more than two pushes of the
81	wheelchair while dribbling, a traveling penalty is called. Even
90	if only the wheel of a player's wheelchair goes out of bounds,
102	the player is out of bounds. A player who lifts out of his or her
117	seat to get a **physical** advantage gets charged with a foul. So
129	does a player whose feet touch the floor.
137	Like wheelchair hockey, each wheelchair basketball player
144	is classified according to his or her ability level.
153	Wheelchair basketball, like wheelchair hockey, takes
159	coordination. Players must use their hands to move their
168	wheelchairs. At the same time, they must be able to handle
179	the ball. 181

Comprehension Check

1. Why does wheelchair basketball take coordination? **Details**

2. Why are sports adapted for wheelchairs? **Cause and Effect**

	Words Read	–	Number of Errors	=	Words Correct Score
First Read		–		=	
Second Read		–		=	

© Macmillan/McGraw-Hill

Name _____

Most authors have a **viewpoint** or **position** that they present to readers. A reader's job is to identify this viewpoint and decide whether to agree. Authors try to persuade readers by using the following devices to explain the basic relationships among ideas.
Parallelism: repeating words, phrases, or grammatical structures.
Comparison: showing how two things are alike.
Causality: showing how one thing leads to another.

Read the passage. Then complete the chart and answer the question.

Just as oceans and mountains challenged past explorers, so have obstacles faced by children with disabilities challenged today's inventors. Modern playground designers seek to create playgrounds that all children can enjoy. In many instances, children with disabilities themselves have helped lead the way to new designs. The children have identified problems and recommended solutions. By working together, young people and designers have made it possible for children of all abilities to enjoy their time in the sun. And like the playgrounds of the past, the new playgrounds are colorful and inviting.

Type of Device	Example Sentence from Passage	What It Shows
Parallelism		
Comparison		
Causality		

What is the author's position? _____

_____

You see printed materials that provide information about the world around you every day. **Everyday communications** have many forms.

Study the descriptions below. Then answer the questions.

Consumer materials	Warranty: guarantees a product or its parts for a period of time
	Product instructions: explain how to operate a product
Directions	Maps explain how to get from one place to another.
Advertisements	Help-wanted ad: explains a particular job and how to apply for it
	Store ad: provides information about the store and its merchandise
Brochure	a small booklet that contains information about a place, service, person, or object
Newsletter	a printed report or letter giving information about a special group or organization

1. What might you read if you were looking for a job? _____

2. Would you read a brochure or a warranty to learn more about a museum exhibit? _____

3. A neighborhood club is planning a Fourth of July parade. What would you read to find out when and where the parade begins? _____

4. What might you read to learn how to operate your new camera?

   _____

5. What would you use to get directions from California to Texas?

   _____

© Macmillan/McGraw-Hill

Name _____

You can figure out the meaning of an unfamiliar word by using **context clues**, the words around the unfamiliar word.

Read each sentence. Use context clues to help you define the boldface word. Then write the letter of the best choice on the line.

1. During the game, my **opponent** was the best player on the other team.

   An opponent is _____.

   a. a competitor   **b.** an ally   **c.** a coach

2. The athletes trained at a high **altitude** because it is much more difficult to run in the mountains.

   Altitude is _____.

   a. an underwater cave   **b.** the height above sea level   **c.** a plateau

3. The winning women's basketball team looked **regal** with their gold medals and flowers on top of the podium.

   Regal means _____.

   a. deprived of food   **b.** serious   **c.** like royalty

4. Joe was accompanied by his guide dog, who **escorted** him into the gymnasium.

   To be escorted is to be _____.

   a. complex   **b.** guided   **c.** called

5. For months the team practiced their **maneuvers**, until the exercises became natural to them.

   Maneuvers are _____.

   a. movements   **b.** schedules   **c.** relationships

Name _____

A. Reading Strategy: Make Connections

You can make connections between or among texts of different genres. Choose a text that you are reading this week. Complete the web by connecting the text that you read with a text of a different genre. Concentrate on making a connection about main idea/theme, author's purpose, or author's perspective.

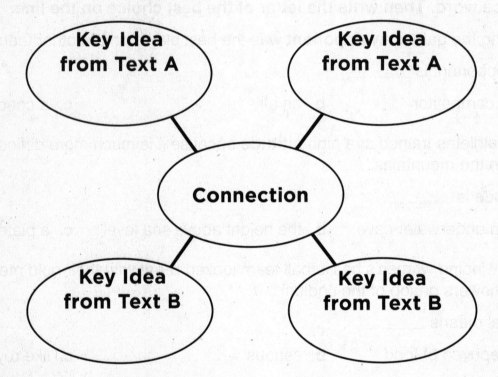

Key Idea from Text A

Key Idea from Text A

Connection

Key Idea from Text B

Key Idea from Text B

B. Independent Reading Log

Choose something you would like to read. After reading, complete the reading log. Be sure to include the main idea or meaning of the text. Keep the details or events in the proper order. You may use your log to talk to others about what you read.

Genre _____

Title _____

Author _____

This Text Is About _____

_____

Name _____

A prefix is a word part that can be added to the beginning of other words or word parts to change the word's meaning. Some prefixes refer to an amount and are called **number prefixes**.

Prefix	Number	Example
uni-	1	unity
bi-	2	bicycle
tri-	3	triceratops
cent-	100	centennial

A. Choose the best prefix for the boldface word. Then write the complete word on the line.

1. The girl put on her soccer _____**form** before the game.

   _____

2. Every _____**meter** counts when carefully measuring the length of a board. _____

3. The _____**cycle** has three wheels. _____

4. Stephanie was _____**lingual** and knew two languages.

   _____

B. Circle the prefix in each word. Then write a definition of the word that is based on the meaning of the prefix.

5. triangle _____

6. universe _____

7. bisect _____

8. centipede _____

9. tripod _____

10. unicorn _____

founding	civilization	shortage	outcast
traditional	strategy	complex	reflected

A. Choose words from the box to complete the sentences below.

1. When fall came, there was no _____ of fruit from the large orchard.

2. The shiny leaves _____ the bright light of the afternoon sun.

3. In history class, we are studying the _____ of our town back in the 1800s.

4. Breeding hybrid fruits and vegetables is _____ work, but eating them is simple.

5. The teacher taught his students to always include everyone and not to

    make anyone feel like an _____.

6. Dusting the plants with flour was part of their _____ to protect the tomato plants from insects.

7. Our _____ holiday dessert is apple pie.

8. Our _____ has a long history of growing grain to feed people and trading the extra grain for other goods.

B. Possible definitions of the vocabulary words are below.
Circle whether the given definition is true or false.

9. T F strategy: a careful plan

10. T F outcast: a well-liked individual

11. T F shortage: an abundance or a large amount

12. T F complex: hard to understand or do

Name _____

The essential message, or **theme**, of a story, is the overall idea or message about life that the author wants readers to understand. To find the theme, look for clues in what happens as a result of the characters' words and actions. This will help you to figure out what the author thinks is a meaningful and important lesson for the readers to apply to their own lives.

Read the passage. Then answer the questions.

Wesley often found new ways of doing things that he liked better than the ordinary ways.

Some of Wesley's ideas helped him prove himself to the other children in the neighborhood. Before Wesley founded Weslandia, the children in the neighborhood had teased him because they did not understand him. Instead of fitting in by imitating the others, Wesley made friends by being himself.

1. Why did the other children tease Wesley? _____

_____

_____

2. Do you think the author believes that imitating other people to get along is a good idea? Explain your answer.

_____

_____

_____

3. What is the theme or message of the story? Explain.

_____

_____

4. Is this theme similar or different from the theme of "Juanita and the Cornstalk"?

_____

_____

Name _____

As you read *Weslandia*, fill in the Theme Chart.

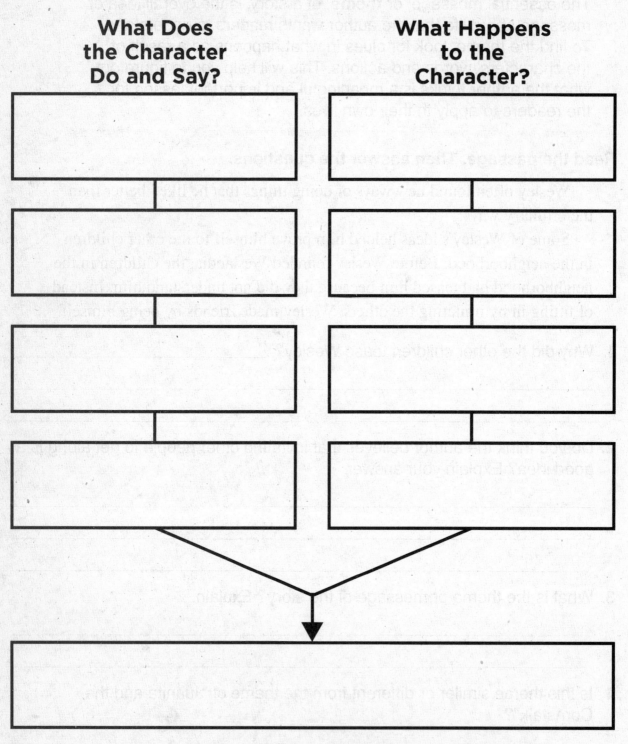

What Does the Character Do and Say?	What Happens to the Character?

How does the information you wrote in the Theme Chart help you generate questions about *Weslandia*?

As I read, I will pay attention to expression and phrasing.

	Two thousand years ago, redwood forests stretched along
8	the Pacific Coast of North America. Today only about
17	four percent of them remain. These survivors live in a narrow
28	band along the foggy coasts of Oregon and northern
37	California. Part of that forest stands just north of San
47	Francisco. This is Muir Woods.
52	The **secluded**, or hidden, setting of Muir Woods is a deep
63	canyon. In this narrow valley, strong winds cannot **buffet**
72	the redwoods.
74	Visitors compare Muir Woods to a cathedral—a silent,
83	dark church with a very high ceiling. The silence of Muir
94	Woods comes from its green carpet of moss that hushes
104	footsteps. It is dark because the trees grow closely together,
114	shutting out most sunlight. The "high ceiling" comes from
123	the tall redwoods. These are the tallest trees in the world.
134	Most grow to be about 200 to 275 feet (61 to 84 m) tall. 143

Comprehension Check

1. How has the population of redwoods changed over the years? **Compare and Contrast**

2. Why can the wind not buffet the redwoods? **Plot**

	Words Read	–	Number of Errors	=	Words Correct Score
First Read		–		=	
Second Read		–		=	

Writers often try to persuade readers to do or believe something. Some writers make **exaggerated** claims, or overstatements, to sell their ideas, products, or services. Others make **contradictory** statements that leave readers wondering which piece of information is true and which is false. Still other writers make **misleading** statements, directing readers to believe something that is not entirely true.

Read the script for a television commercial. Then complete the items that follow.

Announcer: (1) Every child enjoys Fantasy Crunch breakfast cereal. (2) Fantasy Crunch has nothing but good ingredients in it, such as whole grains. (3) Fantasy Crunch contains all the vitamins and minerals that other kids must get from fruits and vegetables, and it's more fun to eat. (4) With its shiny sugar coating, Fantasy Crunch looks pretty in a bowl. (5) Eating Fantasy Crunch for breakfast will make your whole day fantastic!

1. Which part of Sentence 1 is an exaggeration? _____

2. How is Sentence 3 misleading? _____
_____

3. How do Sentences 2 and 4 contradict each other?
_____
_____
_____

4. Why is Sentence 5 an example of an exaggerated statement?
_____

5. Use exaggerated, contradictory, or misleading statements to describe a product of your choice. Exchange descriptions with a classmate, and analyze each other's claims. If necessary, use a separate sheet of paper.
_____

© Macmillan/McGraw-Hill

Name _____

A **hyperlink** is an electronic connection within text on a Web page
that provides direct access to other documents or information.
A **key word** is a specific word that helps you find information.

**Look at the sample online encyclopedia entry. Then answer
the questions.**

| BACK | FORWARD | STOP | REFRESH | HOME | PRINT |

Address: http://www.example.com

Home | Browse | Newsletters | Favorites | Search | | GO

Living things that have parents that are quite different from each
other are call <u>hybrids</u>. People sometimes breed hybrids because they
may have more desirable traits than either of their parents. People often
mate closely related living things on purpose. This process is called
<u>crossbreeding</u>. A crossbreed is a product of mating individuals from
two distinct breeds or varieties of the same <u>species</u>. Crossbreeding has
given us new kinds of plants that resist disease, produce more food on
the same area of land, and are more nutritious.

1. What are the hyperlinks on this page?

_____

2. If you wanted to find out about different cat breeds, where would you type
this information? What key words would you use?

_____

3. If you wanted more information about different species, which hyperlink
could you click on? How do you know?

_____

_____

Name _____

The etymology, or **origin** of a word, can help you remember its definition. You can discover the origin of a word in a dictionary.

patio *n.* courtyard [Sp]

Find each of these words in the dictionary. Next to each word, write which language it comes from.

1. city _____

2. ranch _____

3. athlete _____

4. spaghetti _____

5. samurai _____

6. rocket _____

7. guitar _____

8. kindergarten _____

9. tycoon _____

10. comrade _____

© Macmillan/McGraw-Hill

Name _____

A. Reading Strategy: Make Connections

You can make connections between or among texts of different genres. Choose a text that you are reading this week. Then complete the statements by connecting that text with texts of other genres. Concentrate on making connections about main idea/theme, author's purpose, or author's perspective.

The text I am reading is _____.

It reminds me of _____

because _____.

It also reminds me of _____

because _____.

B. Independent Reading Log

Choose something you would like to read. After reading, complete the reading log. Be sure to include the main idea or meaning of the text. Keep the details or events in the proper order. You may use your log to talk to others about what you read.

Genre_____

Title_____

Author_____

This Text Is About _____

_____

_____

_____

_____

_____

_____

_____

© Macmillan/McGraw-Hill

Some words end with the Latin-derived suffixes **-able** or **-ible**. When they are added as suffixes, they change the word's meaning. Both of these suffixes mean "able to be," "capable of being," "likely to," "worthy of being," "fit for," or "tending to."

A. Think about adding *-able* or *-ible* to complete each word. Write the complete word on the line at the right.

1. cap____   _____

2. invis____   _____

3. poss____   _____

4. us____   _____

5. suit____   _____

B. Add the suffix *-able* or *-ible* to create a new word. Write the new word on the line. Then write a sentence containing that word.

6. break   _____

_____

7. sense   _____

_____

8. convert   _____

_____

9. honor   _____

_____

10. collapse   _____

_____

Name _____

| attraction | emerged | inquire | focused |

A. Replace the underlined word or words in each sentence with a vocabulary word from the box.

1. We <u>concentrated</u> on the waves and nothing else, hoping to see a whale.

    _____

2. The immense blue whale finally <u>rose into view</u> from the water.

    _____

3. If you <u>ask</u> at the library, the librarians can provide several books about whales. _____

4. The beautiful harbor was the town's greatest <u>draw</u> for tourists.

    _____

B. Read each sentence below. Choose the correct meaning of the underlined word. Circle the letter of your answer.

5. The villagers had many <u>discussions</u> before they decided on a plan.

    a. conversations   **b.** problems   **c.** parties

6. The sleeping adult seals were <u>sprawled</u> across the beach as their pups played in the surf.

    a. in motion   **b.** awake and watchful   **c.** lying with limbs spread out

7. When she was frightened, the young child became <u>unreasonable</u> and wouldn't listen to her parents.

    a. foolish and senseless   **b.** happy and cheerful   **c.** easily distracted

8. After the scientists assured them that it was safe to do so, they <u>ventured</u> to touch the whale.

    a. feared   **b.** dared   **c.** planned

When you summarize, you describe the characters, setting, and select the most important plot events, ideas, and details of a story or a text. These descriptions should be organized in your own words.

Read the story. Answer the question that follows each paragraph.

When I was younger, I was very shy. I dreamed of becoming an actor, but I couldn't imagine ever performing in front of others. My mother always told me, "Alma, dreams come true for people who make them come true."

1. What is Alma's problem? _____

_____

For my tenth birthday, I decided to follow my mother's advice. I asked my parents if I could enroll in acting lessons. My parents agreed and signed me up for lessons with Mrs. Parker, an acting coach in our community.

2. What does Alma do to solve her problem? _____

_____

When my mother dropped me off at Mrs. Parker's house, I was so terrified I could hardly say hello. Mrs. Parker put me at ease, though. Before long, I forgot my shyness as I learned to put my heart and mind into different characters.

3. What happens at Mrs. Parker's house? _____

_____

I knew I had overcome my shyness once and for all when I gathered the courage to audition for the school play. I didn't get the lead role, but I did get a supporting role. I plan to audition for more plays. If I keep working hard and practicing, maybe one day you'll see me, Alma Sanchez, on the big screen.

4. How does the story end? _____

_____

Now use your answers to help you write a brief summary.

As you read *The Gri Gri Tree*, fill in the Summarize Chart.

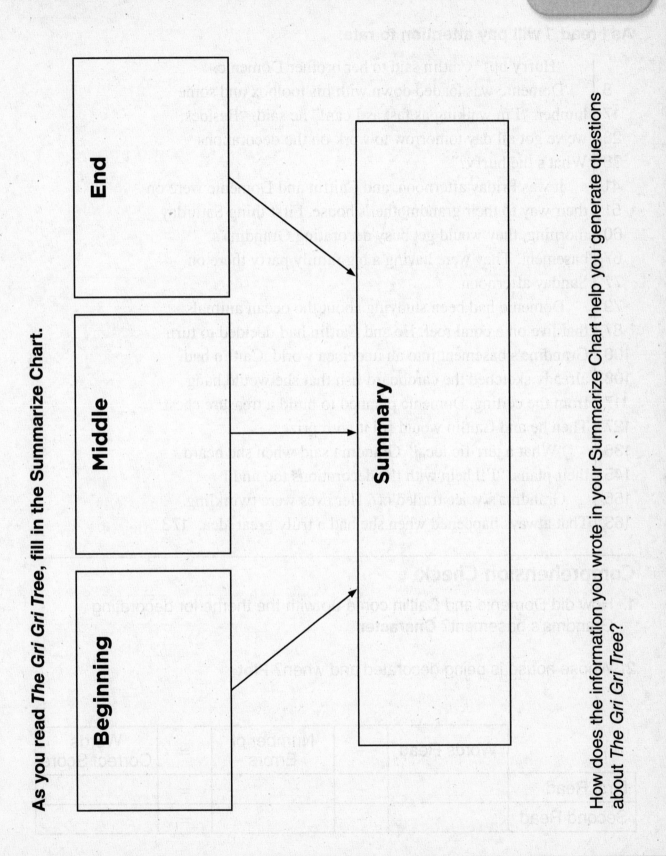

Beginning

Middle

End

Summary

How does the information you wrote in your Summarize Chart help you generate questions about *The Gri Gri Tree*?

Name _____

As I read, I will pay attention to rate.

	"Hurry up!" Caitlin said to her brother Domenic.
8	Domenic was loaded down with his toolbox and some
17	lumber. "I'm walking as fast as I can!" he said. "Besides,
28	we've got all day tomorrow to work on the decorations.
38	What's the hurry?"
41	It was Friday afternoon, and Caitlin and Domenic were on
51	their way to their grandmother's house. First thing Saturday
60	morning, they would get busy decorating Grandma's
67	basement. They were having a big family party there on
77	Sunday afternoon.
79	Domenic had been studying about the ocean animals
87	that live on a coral reef. He and Caitlin had decided to turn
100	Grandma's basement into an undersea world. Caitlin had
108	already sketched the cardboard fish that she would hang
117	from the ceiling. Domenic planned to build a treasure chest.
127	Then he and Caitlin would fill it with prizes.
136	"What a terrific idea!" Grandma said when she heard
145	their plans. "I'll help with the decorations too and I . . . ."
155	Grandma's voice trailed off. Her eyes were twinkling.
163	That always happened when she had a truly great idea. 173

Comprehension Check

1. How did Domenic and Caitlin come up with the theme for decorating Grandma's basement? **Character**

2. Whose house is being decorated and when? **Plot**

	Words Read	−	Number of Errors	=	Words Correct Score
First Read		−		=	
Second Read		−		=	

Name _____

> Sometimes you will read two or more texts that discuss the same
> or similar topic. When this happens you will need to **synthesize**,
> or combine, ideas from the texts. This can be a challenge when
> reading texts of different genres. To synthesize information, look for
> **logical connections** among ideas by considering how the ideas
> across the texts are similar and different.

Read the passages about volcanoes. Then answer the questions.

A Volcano Legend

Native American legends explain volcanic activity in the western United
States. Long ago, there were two chiefs. The Chief of the Below World,
Llao, stood on top of Mount Mazama in Oregon. Skell, the Chief of the
Above World, stood on top of Mount Shasta in California. One night, the
chiefs hurled fiery rocks at each other. One of Skell's volleys injured Llao,
who fell back into the mountain and created a big hole. After filling with
water, the big hole became known as Crater Lake.

Volcanoes

Volcanoes are mountains that have been formed by the eruption of
magma, or molten rock. Eruptions occur when magma pushes its way up
and through Earth's surface. Eruptions can be loud or quiet. Quiet or not,
volcanic eruptions can be destructive. Eruptions can cause landslides, rock
falls, and fires.

1. How are the passages alike? _____

2. How are the passages different? _____

   _____

   _____

3. Which passage uses the most recent information? Explain your answer.

   _____

   _____

A line **graph** shows how data changes over time.

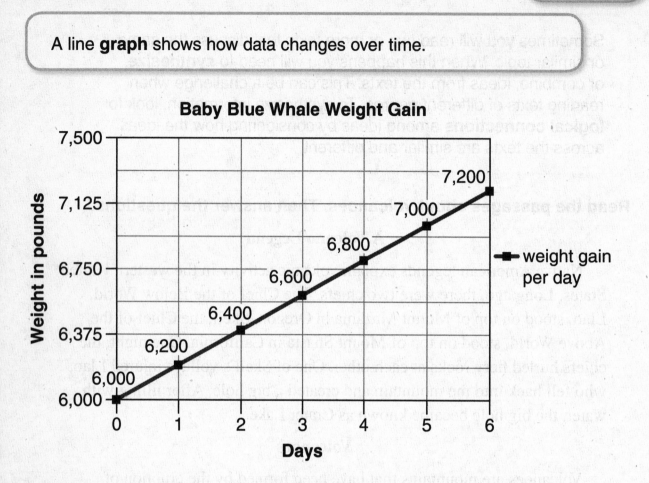

Baby Blue Whale Weight Gain

7,200

7,000

6,800

6,600

6,400

6,200

6,000

weight gain
per day

Weight in pounds: 7,500, 7,125, 6,750, 6,375, 6,000, 6,000

Days: 0 1 2 3 4 5 6

The graph above shows the weight gain of a blue whale for one
week. Use the graph to answer the questions below.

1. What is the title of this graph?

_____

2. How much does the blue whale weigh at the beginning of the study?

_____

3. How much weight does a blue whale gain per day? _____

4. How much will a blue whale weigh on day 7? How did you get your answer?

_____

_____

_____

Name _____

A word root is part of a word that does not usually stand by itself as a base word. Prefixes or suffixes are attached to a word root. Many word roots are Latin in origin. If you know the meaning of the **Latin root**, you can figure out the meaning of an unfamiliar word.

Read each sentence. Write the meaning of each boldface word on the line provided. Use the table of Latin roots below to help you determine each definition.

Root	Meaning
duct	lead, take, bring
medius	middle
fortis	strong
tract	pull or draw

1. Does water **contract** or expand when it freezes? _____

_____

2. The boys could not agree, so a **mediator** was called in to hear both

arguments. _____

3. The **aqueducts** brought water into the ancient city. _____

_____

4. Let's make a **deduction** based on the facts we know._____

_____

5. The troops **fortified** the town in preparation for the enemy invasion.

_____

Name _____

A. Reading Strategy: Make Connections

You can make connections between or among texts of different genres.
Choose a text that you are reading this week. Complete the activity by
connecting that text with texts of other genres.

Freewrite for a few minutes about ideas from the text that you are reading.

_____

_____

_____

Freewrite for a few minutes about ideas from texts that remind you of
what you are reading.

_____

_____

_____

Use your freewriting to make connections among the texts. Concentrate on
making connections about main idea/theme, author's purpose, or author's
perspective. Also, give details from the texts to support your connections.

_____

_____

B. Independent Reading Log

Choose something you would like to read. After reading, complete the reading
log. Be sure to include the main idea or meaning of the text. Keep the details
or events in the proper order. You may use your log to talk to others about what
you read.

Genre_____

Title_____

Author _____

This Text Is About _____

_____